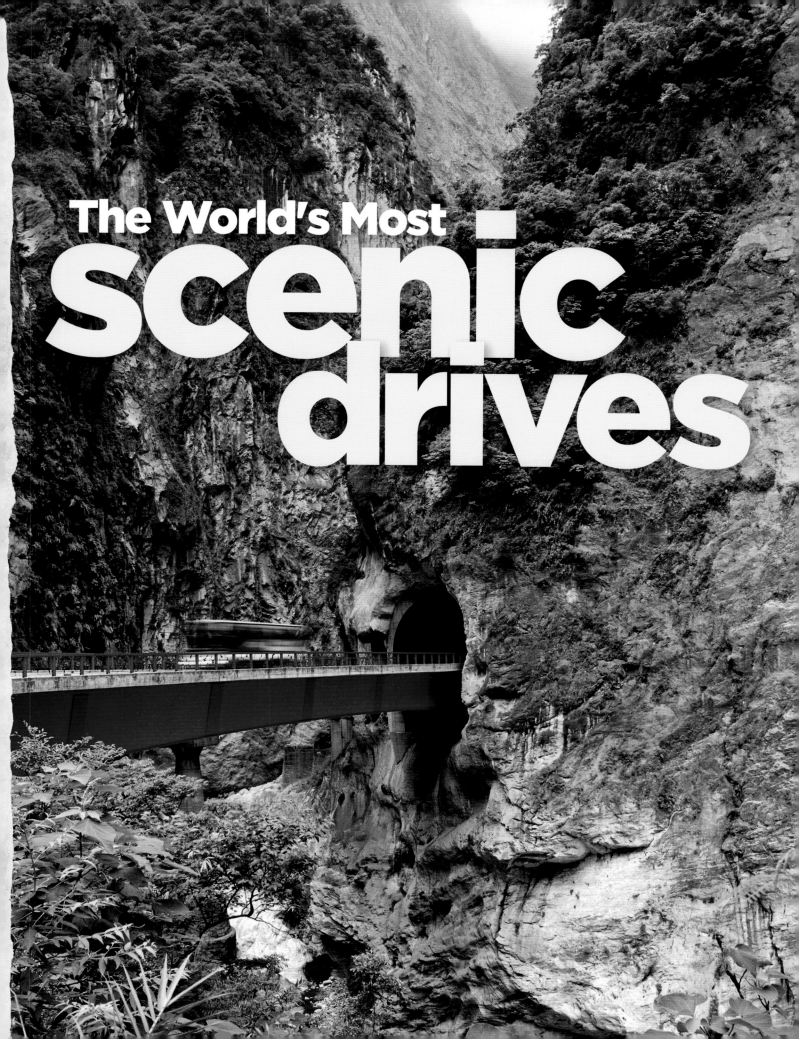

The World's Most
scenic
drives

Previous: Following the lip of the Taroko Gorge in Taiwan, the Central Cross Island Highway passes through 38 tunnels and around countless twists and turns.

Below: Quaint cottages are a common sight in the picturesque Cotswold region of England.

The World's Most
scenic
drives

101 spectacular trips

NATIONAL GEOGRAPHIC
WASHINGTON, D.C.

CONTENTS

World Map **6**

Drives by Country **126**

drives **1-25**

coastal
wanderings 8

Skirting the water's edge these drives take you to quaint fishing villages, idyllic islands, and splendid seashores.

drives **26-45**

cities
and beyond 38

City lights and scenic surroundings lure you down urban boulevards and suburban streets.

drives **46-74**

backroad
rambles 62

Wide-open spaces around every bend have these local roads begging to be explored.

drives **75-101**

mountain
meanders 96

The road demands as much attention as the views as you chase the horizon over soaring mountains.

A safari vehicle drives through the deep floodwaters of the Okavango Delta in Botswana.

53 Seward Highway, p. 72

75 Yukon Circle, p. 98

16 The Ring Road, Iceland, p. 25

Alaska (U.S.)

NORTH AMERICA

CANADA

46 Icefields Parkway, p. 64

27 A Calgary Circle, p. 41

4 The Western Isles, Washington, p. 13

51 To-the-Sun Road, Montana, p. 70

12 Green Gables Shore, Prince Edward Island, p. 23

57 The Ring of Kerry, Ireland, p. 78

5 Pacific Grace, Oregon, p. 14

47 Newfoundland Fun, p. 65

62 Following Lewis and Clark, North and South Dakota, p. 83

26 East from Montreal, p. 40

59 Indre River Ride, France, p. 80

77 Beartooth Highway, Montana and Wyoming, p. 100

1 Cape Breton Circle, p. 10

48 Riding Vermont 100, Vermont, p. 66

2 Maine's Bold Coast, Maine, p. 11

15 On John Steinbeck's Heels: Monterey County, California., p. 23

14 Following Twain: Hannibal and Environs, Mo., p. 23

13 Concord's Literary Route, Mass., p. 23

90 Country Roads, Portugal, p. 112

6 Big Sur Coast, California, p. 16

3 Old King's Highway, Mass., p. 12

52 Death Valley Drive, California, p. 71

28 Down Fifth Avenue, N.Y., p. 42

84 Strongholds of the Middle Ages, Portugal, p. 108

30 Sunset Boulevard, California, p. 45

UNITED STATES

76 Blue Ridge Parkway, Virginia and North Carolina, p. 99

19 Spain's Secret Coast, Spain, p. 29

55 Baja Expedition, p. 75

50 Route 66, N. Mex. and Ariz., p. 69

49 Chattahoochee!, Georgia, p. 67

41 Beyond Fès, p. 55

MOROCCO

54 East End Drive, p. 74

29 Miami to the Keys, Fla., p. 43

Atlantic Ocean

7 Hana's Highway, p. 17

Hawaii (U.S.)

78 Cuba's Southwest, p. 101

MEXICO

63 Path of the Conquerors, Yucatán, p. 83

CUBA

80 Cordillera Samaná, p. 104

79 The Panoramic Route, p. 102

JAMAICA

8 Pirate Path, p. 18

DOM. REP.

9 Basse-Terre Loop, p. 20

Puerto Rico (U.S.)

Guadeloupe (FR.)

Pacific Ocean

10 Coastal Adventure, p. 21

56 Caribbean Wild, p. 77

COSTA RICA

81 North of Penonomé, p. 105

31 Azuero Experience, p. 46

PANAMA

82 Coffee Country, p. 106

COLOMBIA

EQUATOR

SOUTH AMERICA

PERU

BRAZIL

32 Pan-Am Highway, p. 47

MAP KEY

drive number — drive name — page number

101 Osado Skyline Drive, p. 124

■ Symbols are located at drive starting points.

11 The Green Coast, p. 22

33 Along the Salta Loop, p. 48

ARGENTINA

Scale at Equator:

0 — 1,000 — 2,000 mi

0 — 1,000 — 2,000 km

83 Pure Patagonia, p. 107

Arctic Ocean

88 Sperrin Mountains, Ireland, p. 109

17 Applecross Route, Scotland, p. 26

36 Glasgow to St. Andrews, Central Belt, Scotland, p. 51

58 A Cotswolds Loop, England, p. 79

18 Northern Thrills, Norway, p. 27

EUROPE

RUSSIA

89 North York Moors, England, p. 111

35 London by Bus, England, p. 51

34 The Tulip Route, Neth., p. 50

94 Looping Lovely Lakes, Switz., p. 117

39 Moscow's Golden Ring, p. 53

60 Romantic Road Trip, Germany, p. 81

95 Northern Bohemia, Czech Republic, p. 118

85 Langhe Valley, Italy, p. 108

61 The Castle Route, Czech Republic, p. 82

96 Rural Maramures, Romania, p. 119

93 The Alpine Road, Germany, p. 115

92 A "Grand Canyon", France, p. 114

66 Transylvania Spin, Romania, p. 84

86 Classic Wine Road, Plesivica, Croatia, p. 108

38 Bosporus Tour, p. 51

100 The Old Silk Road, p. 123

101 Osado Skyline Drive, p. 124

JAPAN

20 Three Riviera Roads, Fr., p. 30

21 Amalfi Charms, Italy, p. 31

TURKEY

91 Along High Hills, Spain, p. 113

37 Out of Athens, Attica, Greece, p. 51

67 The Peloponnese, Greece, p. 85

CHINA

Pacific

99 Above Zegzel Gorge, p. 122

98 Sicilian Loop, Italy, p. 121

64 Via Appia Antica, Italy, p. 83

72 Taroko Gorge, p. 92

TAIWAN

Ocean

97 Into Chianti Country, Italy, p. 120

73 Driving Sai Kung, p. 93

40 A West Bank Loop, p. 54

EGYPT

42 Along a Mideast Coast, p. 56

OMAN

INDIA

70 Driving the DMZ, p. 89

71 Cordillera Terraces, p. 90

43 Discovering Goa, p. 58

AFRICA

65 Driving the Mandarin Road, p. 83

VIETNAM

PHILIPPINES

23 A Chennai Spin, p. 34

CAMBODIA

44 Phnom Penh Ride, p. 59

EQUATOR

69 Serengeti Safari, p. 88

TANZANIA

Indian

Ocean

68 Wild Okavango, p. 87

BOTSWANA

AUSTRALIA

SOUTH AFRICA

87 Wheatfields and Vineyards, Swartland, p. 108

22 The Garden Route, p. 32

45 The Pacific Highway, p. 60

24 Great Ocean Road, p. 35

25 Coastal East Cape, p. 37

NEW ZEALAND

74 Driving the Catlins, p. 95

coast
wanderings

Australia's Great Ocean Road by Apollo Bay provides a view of the renowned Twelve Apostles.

CANADA

1

cape breton circle

Spectacular scenic views • Seductive hideaways • Plentiful wildlife

Experience the Cabot Trail's thrilling landscapes, from moody highlands to headlands plunging to the sea. Start in lively Baddeck, where Alexander Graham Bell famously had a home and lab.

Head north into salmon country (the Middle River lures many an angler) and stop by the Margaree Salmon Museum, in an old schoolhouse. Wind along the river valley to the coast, where the scene becomes more rugged and the place-names more French. You can't miss Joe's Garden of Scarecrows—110 of them—in Cap LeMoine. Farther on is Chéticamp, gateway to the highlands.

Cape Breton Highlands National Park, with a worthwhile 66-mile (106 km) drive of its own, is the rugged roof of Nova Scotia. Continue inland to Cape North and then back to the coast. Take a scenic detour at White Point. The rewards: stunning views, seductive hideaways, and fishing villages. Drive on to the Ingonish area. The Cape Smokey Lodge offers a 20-minute chairlift ride. From here it is about a 50-mile (80 km) drive to South Gut St. Anns, which was settled by Highland Scots.

travelwise

Start Baddeck **End** South Gut St. Anns **Distance** 186 miles (299 km)
Road Trans-Canada 105
Insider Tip The Normaway Inn hosts live music and dance on Friday night (June, September, October) and Wednesday night (July and August).

Cabot Trail gives a show of autumn colors curving along the coast of Nova Scotia.

Morning light shines on the Otter Cliffs at Acadia National Park, Maine (left). Atlantic puffins perch on Machias Seal Island in the Gulf of Maine (right).

maine's bold coast

Crashing surf • Memorable Americana • Peaceful fishing villages

Your first "oh wow" moment takes place some 25 miles (40 km) into the trip. Less than a mile from Winter Harbor turn right for a side trip to Schoodic Point, a 2,266-acre (917 ha) preserve with a 6-mile (9.6 km) drive along the granite shores of the Schoodic Peninsula, with mountain views, hiking trails, and tidal pools.

At Bartlett Maine Estate Winery on Maine 186 you'll find fruit wines and brandies. In terms of area towns, Cherryfield is billed as the "blueberry capital of the world," while Jonesport and Beals are venerable boatbuilding centers. Nearby is Fort O'Brien State Historic Site, a stone's throw from the first naval battle of the Revolution. Close by is Jasper Beach with its irresistible pebbles of jasper and rhyolite.

Must-sees at the end of the trip are Reversing Falls, the Old Sow Whirlpool (one of the world's largest), and the Moosehorn National Wildlife Refuge (northernmost in a chain of migratory bird refuges that extends from Maine to Florida).

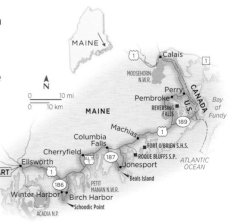

travelwise

Start Ellsworth **End** Calais **Distance** 197 miles (317 km)
Roads East U.S. 1, Maine 186, U.S. 1, Maine 187, Maine 189
Don't Miss Freshwater swimming at Roque Bluffs State Park • The Bay of Fundy's extreme tides • The town of Perry: midway point between the Equator and the North Pole

Cape Cod Highland Lighthouse on Cape Cod National Seashore

MASSACHUSETTS

old king's highway

Culinary delights • Classic villages • Majestic dunelands

In historic Sandwich—about 10 minutes east of Sagamore—take in the renowned colored 19th-century glass at the Sandwich Glass Museum. Domestic architecture, including small 17th-century saltbox houses and classically proportioned Georgian federal-style homes, dot the route. Among the grandest: the Captain Bangs Hallet House in Yarmouth Port.

Hikers and cyclists flock to Cape Cod Rail Trail, which begins in Dennis and ends in Wellfleet, where a wildlife sanctuary hugs the bay (there's also oceanfront in Wellfleet). At North Truro, 7.5 miles (12 km) north of Wellfleet, bear right past Pilgrim Lake to Province Lands, a section of the national seashore with paths winding through dunelands fragrant with beach plum and bayberry to a fine beach.

End up at the tip of Cape Cod at flamboyant Provincetown, a bustling haven of arts, crafts, and cuisine.

travelwise

Start Sagamore   **End** Provincetown   **Distance** 59 miles (95 km)
Roads North Massachusetts 6A, U.S. 6
Insider Tip The town of Brewster, filled with 19th-century sea captains' homes, boasts a wealth of good antiques shops along Main Street. The Brewster Historical Society holds an annual Open Air Antiques Fair in late June.

the western isles

Maritime culture • Idyllic islands • Abundant wildlife

It's tough to break away from stupendous Seattle, but it's worth taking a car ferry across Puget Sound to Bremerton, whose impressive seafaring history is reflected in its naval museum. Head north through Keyport, another naval town. For a change of pace, Norwegian culture is the leitmotif in the old town of Poulsbo. Get up close and personal with sea anemones (and more) at the Marine Science Center.

Continue north, passing various maritime landmarks, including Fort Worden State Park's 19th-century coastal gun emplacements and Port Townsend's Marine Center and pretty pastel-hued Victorian houses. From here catch the ferry to Whidbey Island and drive north to Coupeville, a town with more than 50 National Historic Reserve structures.

Head west past popular Deception Pass State Park (hiking, beaches, lakes). Cross Fidalgo Island and take the Anacortes Ferry to Friday Harbor, a San Juan Islands entry point.

travelwise

Start Seattle **End** Friday Harbor **Distance** 88 miles (142 km)
Roads North Washington 303, 3, 104, U.S. 101, several local roads, Washington 20; the route includes three ferries
Insider Tip In the sweet town of Coupeville, the cozy Oystercatcher restaurant is a favorite for its fresh and delicious regional fare; save room for dessert.

An orca whale leaps out of the water in the Pacific Ocean.

5

pacific grace

Glorious ocean views • Seaside forests • Coastal dunes

Driftwood-dotted beaches, thick rain forests, arty towns, a wealth of wildlife, and spectacular dunes punctuate this grand drive. Enjoy a taste of history early on: the Columbia River Maritime Museum's dugout canoes, Lewis and Clark National Historical Park, and the 19th-century lighthouse in Ecola State Park. The town of Tillamook is famous for its cheddar (perfect with Oregon Cabernet).

Just before the small community of Oceanside, stop on the bluff on the north edge of town to scan Three Arch Rocks National Wildlife Refuge. About an hour before the halfway point of the drive, visit the threatened silverspot butterfly at the Cascade Head Preserve, brown pelicans near Siletz Bay, and the gray whales off the coast near the Yaquina Head Lighthouse.

The Darlingtonia State Wayside's boardwalk leads through bogs thick with carnivorous cobra lilies.

The town of Bandon is best known for its coastal rock formations and September cranberry festival.

travelwise

Start Astoria **End** Bandon
Distance 264 miles (425 km)
Road South U.S. 101
Insider Tip Pick up a jar of mayonnaise and some steamed local Dungeness crab—sweet and meaty. There's no better lunch or snack.

Yaquina Head Lighthouse, working since 1873, overlooks the coast of Newport, Oregon.

14

6

big sur coast

Fabled coastline • Dramatic cliffs • Mellow hillsides

Among your starting city's lures, the Monterey Bay Aquarium swims to the top of the list. Three miles (5 km) south, Carmel-by-the-Sea warrants a stroll along its quaint gallery- and shop-filled streets. Farther south is Point Lobos State Reserve with tide pools, hiking trails, and migrating whales (December through April).

Next up: Big Sur, the fabled 90-mile (145 km) stretch of land and sea magic. In the spotlight are soaring redwoods, cliffs plunging straight into the ocean, sand dunes, parks, beaches, and—a short trail walk away in Julia Pfeiffer Burns State Park—McWay Falls, which pour into a picturesque cove.

The southern stretch of Big Sur clings to a precipitous coastline before easing into hills and pastureland. You'll see Piedras Blancas Light Station and, after a spell away from the Pacific, the town of San Simeon, staging area for the 5-mile (8 km) bus ride to Hearst Castle. The estate (visits by reservation) features a 115-room house.

Farther on as you close in on Morro Bay and its signature turban-shaped rock, pause in the colony of Harmony, where you can watch artists at work.

travelwise

Start Monterey   **End** Morro Bay   **Distance** 123 miles (198 km)
Road South on California Highway 1
Insider Tip Big Sur's popular ocean-view Nepenthe Restaurant (great burgers and fries) once turned away John F. Kennedy for being barefoot.

A stand-up paddleboarder wades into the Pacific Ocean's lapping waves at sunset.

Lush landscapes highlight the natural beauty of Hawaii on the road to Hana.

hana's highway

Authentic Hawaii • Scenic and serpentine route • Lava-covered seashores

You'll cross 56 mostly one-lane bridges and navigate 617 turns on this slow-going trip—the better to take in waterfalls and a rugged lava coastline. The first—and last—notable town is Paia. Two miles (3 km) on is windsurfing hot spot Hookipa.

Between the tiny towns of Huelo and Kailua, look for roadside stands selling guava and mango. The tree with the colorfully streaked bark? Rainbow eucalyptus. Watch for waterfalls. Revisit Jurassic Park at the Garden of Eden Botanical Gardens and Arboretum; portions of the movie were shot here.

Picnic, swim, and admire the plant life at the Keanae Arboretum, just off the main road. Between Wailua and Puaa Kaa State Wayside Park you'll pass Waikani Falls, a good picnic locale. Next stop is Waianapanapa State Park, with a dramatic lava shoreline and a black-sand beach. Camping and cabin overnighting are available by permit. And—finally—the fun town of Hana.

travelwise

Start Kahului Airport, Maui **End** Hana **Distance** 53 miles (85 km)
Roads Northeast Hawaii 36, Hawaii 360
Insider Tip Those in search of the 1960s will find it in the town of Paia, which went psychedelic decades ago and never got over it. On a practical note, this is the last place on the route to gas up.

JAMAICA

8

pirate path

Caribbean vistas • Historic pirate
haunts • Alluring island villages

A faded Red Stripe beer sign just outside
Port Royal pegs the old city as the place
"where the buccaneers drank their beer."
It's a fine sentiment for the start of a glorious island road trip that, through green
savannas, sugarcane fields, and mountains,
can't help but recall the likes of Captain
Jack Sparrow. Called the "wickedest city in
Christendom," Port Royal was decimated
in a 1692 earthquake. Today it's a quiet
fishing town. In St. Peter's Church is a silver Communion service said to have been
donated by the city's infamous Captain
Henry Morgan, a pirate to the core.

   Drive along the Palisadoes to Kingston,
Jamaica's capital.

   Past the resort town of Negril, on the
top of Round Hill, are the remains of a fort
built in the early 18th century to protect
the harbor from pirates.

   Though the buccaneer-related sights
thin out as you continue east to Port
Antonio, the beauty of the Blue Mountain
views—and the authentic jerk pork in laid-
back Boston Bay—more than compensate.

travelwise

Start Port Royal **End** Port Royal
Distance 380 miles (612 km)
Roads A2, Highway 2000, A1
Insider Tip The best way to experience
the island music—the cultural back-
bone of Jamaica—is at the July Reggae
Sumfest in Montego Bay.

Small, colorful boats sit in still waters near Ocho Rios.

Rolling hills covered with tropical flowers perfectly frame the bright blue bay of Deshaies.

GUADELOUPE

9

basse-terre loop

Mountain scenery • Coastal adventures • Natural wonders

A clockwise circuit out of Pointe-à-Pitre includes spectacular rain forests, mountains, and waterfalls. The Cascade aux Écrevisses (crayfish) is the first wonder along the way, followed by the Maison de la Forêt, with flora, fauna, and geology displays (in French) and a wide choice of strolls and hikes.

After a hairpin descent to the coast at Mahaut you can detour south to Plage de Malendure for a glass-bottom-boat ride or continue on to Maison du Cacao. At the Maison du Bois, just up the coast, you'll see how the local wood has been transformed into all manner of usable objects.

The drive continues past the fishing village of Deshaies and the broad bay at Grande Anse, graced by one of Guadeloupe's finest beaches. Continue on to the Musée du Rhum—a celebration of three centuries' worth of rum making in the Caribbean—before picking up the Route N2 for a swift return to Pointe-à-Pitre.

travelwise

Start Pointe-à-Pitre   **End** Pointe-à-Pitre   **Distance** 58 miles (93 km)
Roads Routes N1, D23, N2
Don't Miss A hike through one of Maison de la Forêt's well-maintained trails
• Col des Mamelles, the highest point along the route • A museum visit: You can explore the local rum, wooden furniture and utensils, or the rich history of cocoa

coastal adventure

Beautiful beaches • Sublime views • Rugged coastal road

Clamber over mountainous headlands to hidden beaches, fishing villages, and wild jungle. Begin in the offbeat hamlet Sámara, fill up the gas tank, and drive to your first landmark, Playa Carrillo, a favorite among sportfishermen. Ridley and leatherback turtles populate nearby Playa Islita.

Spiral down to Islita, home to an open-air art museum, then climb again to Punta Barranquilla, the narrow dirt road clinging magically to the mountainside. Farther south, Playa Bejuco and Playa Coyote are prime turtle-sighting spots.

The going really gets tricky at San Francisco de Coyote. Unpaved Highway 152 links San Francisco to Highway 21 and continues on to Río Jabillo, which you must ford. No problem unless the road is flooded. The ubiquitous mango groves shelter egrets, snakes, turtles, and crocodiles.

Enjoy a restaurant pit stop in the hamlet of Betel. From there rough track claws over Punta Pochote to surfing hot spots Playa Santa Teresa and Malpaís.

travelwise

Start Sámara **Finish** Malpaís **Distance** 57 miles (92 km)
Road East Highway 150
Don't Miss Playa Carrillo—the sliver of white-sand beach and the fishing hamlet • Playa Coyote and its promise of jungle wildlife • The bellows of howler monkeys and screeching toucans along Playa Bongo, accessible only at low tide

Horses offer a more leisurely view of Punta Islita.

World famous Copacabana Beach, Rio de Janeiro, affords beachgoers simultaneous views of blue oceans and green mountains.

the green coast

Fine beaches • Lush green mountains • Brazilian botanicals

This slice of Brazil's Costa Verde offers the best of many worlds. After taking the cog train to Corcovado, ascending to Sugar Loaf via cable car, strolling Ipanema beach, hiking in the national park, and visiting the botanic garden, make your way southwest.

Drive past the fishing village of Mangaratiba, a port that saw a wealth of gold and coffee exports in the 18th century, and get ready to park at Angra dos Reis, where you'll ferry to a slice of paradise: Ilha Grande is a 74-square-mile (192 sq km) ecotourist island with dazzling beaches (hidden coves to surfing locales), lush hillsides (nice for hikes), and no cars (yes, no cars!).

With its cobblestone streets, harbor, restaurants, nightlife, and nearby beaches and waterfalls, Paraty is a good place to end up—and stay for a couple of days.

travelwise

Start Rio de Janeiro **End** Paraty **Distance** 150 miles (241 km)
Road BR-101, ferry between Angra dos Reis and Ilha Grande
Insider Tip The hotel Caso do Bicho Preguica is an idyllic spot to spend a few days and nights of tropical quietude on sun-teased waters. If you want to get busy, you can kayak, hike, swim, or enjoy a cold beer and fresh shrimp with Ilha Grande in the background.

literary roads

12
Green Gables Shore, Prince Edward Island, Canada

Motor along the northern coast of one of the prettiest sections of Canada with Anne as your leitmotif. Make a stop at the Green Gables House (the old farm site that inspired Lucy Maud Montgomery to write what would become the best-selling novel *Anne of Green Gables*) and be sure to experience a stroll or hike in PEI National Park. Be sure to have afternoon tea at Dalvay by the Sea, a national historic site and oceanfront resort.

www.tourismpei.com

13
Concord's Literary Route, Massachusetts

The town is best known for its ties to the Revolutionary War, but Concord and environs formed a thrilling nexus of 19th-century literary talent as well. Orchard House, where Louisa May Alcott wrote—and set—*Little Women,* is now a tribute to her life and most famous novel. The Old Manse was once home to Nathaniel Hawthorne. Thoreau's beloved Walden Pond is a stone's throw away. Also worth a visit is the Concord Museum, which is home to one of the most extensive collections of Americana in the country.

www.concordchamberof commerce.org

14
Following Twain: Hannibal and Environs, Missouri

Experience the landscapes of Mark Twain's books, beginning with the boyhood home of this American icon and moving on to the interactive New Mark Twain Museum, which displays 15 original Norman Rockwell paintings. A mile (1.6 km) south of Hannibal is Mark Twain Cave, the model of the cave in *The Adventures of Tom Sawyer*. In Riverside Park, overlooking the Mississippi, the river that shaped Twain's life, is a statue of the great writer.

www.marktwaincountry.com

15
On John Steinbeck's Heels: Monterey County, California

Begin in the author's hometown, Salinas. Drop by the Roosevelt School (*East of Eden*'s West End School), then head south, stopping at Soledad (the setting for *Of Mice and Men*), King City (*The Red Pony),* and Jolon (*To a God Unknown*). Most well known, Monterey's Cannery Row was the setting for the book of the same name as well as *Tortilla Flat*. Along with several real-life *East of Eden* characters, Steinbeck is buried at Garden of Memories Cemetery in Salinas.

www.steinbeck.org

Historic waterfront district Cannery Row, Monterey, California

the ring road

Frozen lava outcrops • Icebergs • Wild pansies

On this dazzling trip around Iceland's rim, surprises are the norm: icebergs floating below a bridge . . . wind like you've never felt before . . . volcanic craters elegantly surrounded by moss . . . cloud-girdled mountains . . . fermented shark meat (on many a menu) . . . turf-covered churches . . . small horses with magical manes . . . sulfur-infused steam rising from impossibly blue pools (yes, go ahead, take a dip).

Drive Iceland's Ring Road—completed in 1974 and still unpaved in parts—by heading north out of the country's modern capital, Reykjavík. The landscape quickly evolves into gentle green (farmland) backdropped by gentle mountains (snowcapped) before the road detours around Hvalfjördur ("whale fjord").

Hvammstangi, a small village beside a north-coast fjord, is a good place to enjoy a meal and spend your first night. Pressing on, you'll come to arty Akureyri, northern Iceland's main metropolis. An hour's drive east lands you in Mývatn, an area that marks the volcanic boundary between Europe and North America.

Toward the end of the trip, linger in Hveragerði—an eco-haven town—and visit the geothermal-heated greenhouses, some with cafés. Yes, one more surprise.

travelwise

Start Reykjavík **End** Reykjavík **Distance** 832 miles (1,339 km)
Road Iceland Route 1
Insider Tip Schedule your journey to coincide with the summer solstice, when daylight goes on and on. Plan on a week-long trip, and take advantage of the charming farmhouse accommodations along the way.

**Opposite: A waterfall spills off the dramatic southern Iceland landscape along the Ring Road.
Below: Icelandic horses gather in a pasture.**

applecross route

Natural beauty • Mesmerizing scenery • Famed lakesides

Don't the let the twists and turns of Scotland's highest road, the Bealach Na Ba, give you pause; navigating the attention-demanding byway is a small price to pay for the fine rewards—from breathtaking views to (now here's a surprise) boat-fresh seafood as well as smoked salmon.

With its myriad hiking trails, Torridon Mountains cry out for a hike. Afterward, sit back and enjoy the ride. In Shieldaig, stop for some sustenance at the Tigh an Eilean Hotel. The road then skirts the coast of the Applecross Peninsula, winding dizzily along the shore of Loch Torridon before curving south along the Inner Sound and dramatic vistas over the islands of Rona and Raasay.

The whitewashed village of Applecross, a clutch of quaint cottages, is great for a stroll as well as the starting point for longer walks. In the wings? Get ready for the most exhilarating portion of the ride. From Applecross, the Bealach Na Ba Road climbs clouds-ward, seducing with view point after view point. But do remember to watch the road, which is single-lane in parts. The descent will make you think of roller-coaster rides. By the time you reach Lochcarron you will be ready to unwind.

travelwise

Start Loch Torridon Visitor Center   **End** Lochcarron   **Distance** 50 miles (80 km)
Road A896
Insider Tip Stop at Lochcarron Weavers shop for all things tartan—from teddy bears to kilts, caps to blankets. The shop is a 5-minute drive west of Lochcarron.

The famous red-roofed cottage by Loch Shieldaig sits in the Torridon Mountains, Scotland.

Sunlight starts to filter into the hole at Torghatten, Norway, looking out into the open sea.

northern thrills

Arctic Circle crossing • Archetypal fjords • Hikes and views

Here's a drive, one of the best on Earth, that literally places you on top of the world as well as on a few ferry boats. Norway's Kystriksveien—translation: "coastal route"—takes you to the north side of the Arctic Circle (via a 60-minute car ferry trip from Kilboghamn). But let's start at the beginning.

As is the case with many inland towns, the journey's departure point—Steinkjer—is actually connected to the Norwegian Sea by a fjord; a ferry carries you and your car across. Back on the road, you'll soon pass Namsos (an old lumber town) and the Namsen (a river known for great salmon fishing).

Some of the route's most breathtaking vistas come into view as you reach the Sjonfjellet Mountains. After your Arctic Circle crossing and en route to Bodø, stop and gape at Svartisen, one of the country's largest glaciers.

travelwise

Start Steinkjer **End** Bodø **Distance** 446 miles (718 km)
Roads Routes 17, 769, 770, 80
Don't Miss Shopping for local crafts; you'll find, for instance, a textile and ceramics workshop just past the hamlet of Berg • The 20-minute hike up Torghatten Mountain, the most famous landmark on Norway's coast • Sea kayaking outside the port city of Bodø

spain's secret coast

Rugged countryside • Picturesque beaches • Quaint fishing villages

Start out on foot in Níjar, a village of whitewashed houses huddled against the slopes of the Sierra de Alhamilla. Be sure to see the ornate Mudejar ceiling in the 15th-century church. Back behind the wheel, follow signs to Almería and San Isidro. Don't get onto the highway; drive through the underpass.

Eight miles (13 km) farther is Parque Natural de Cabo de Gata-Níjar, a vast reserve that enjoys the driest weather in Europe. It's a great place for birding. The road winds to Boca de los Frailes and the old mill at Pozo de los Frailes. Follow signs to Playa de los Genoveses, a popular sandy beach. Just beyond is Playa de Monsul, signaled by an enormous sand dune. Monsul has a great view south to the Cabo de Gata lighthouse. These beaches have been locations for many a movie, including *Indiana Jones and the Last Crusade.*

Forgo San José, a tourist resort, in favor of real-deal fishing villages, such as Isleta del Moro. Drink in views en route to Rodalquilar (where you can see the ruined remains of an old gold mine) and beyond to Agua Amarga, a bay-nestled fishing village with restaurants and crafts shops. Return to the main road and turn right up into the hills. As you descend, you can't miss the cement works that introduce the little resort of Carboneras with its long palm-lined beach and marina.

Beyond that is pure drama: Playa la Galera is backed by sheer cliffs. The views here are nothing short of stupendous. Descending through rugged mountains, the road traverses the pretty village of Sopalmo and soon passes the fort of Macenas. Finish up at the hill village of Mojácar.

travelwise

Start Níjar **End** Mojácar **Distance** 70 miles (113 km)
Roads Local roads
Don't Miss Artisan crafts—baskets, rugs, ceramics—in the town of Níjar • Lunch in the tiny fishing village of Isleta del Moro • Rodalquilar, an old gold mine village

Opposite: Abandoned gold mines of Rodalquilar   Below: Agua Amarga, a traditional seaside Andalusian village

Colorful buildings surround the harbor in Villefranche-sur-Mer on the French Riviera.

FRANCE

three riviera roads

Colorful towns • Top-drawer shops • Mediterranean magic

Built in the 1860s to bring gamblers to the new Monte Carlo casino, the Basse Corniche opened up fishing villages that have evolved into seaside resorts. First up is pretty Villefranche-sur-Mer, whose Chapelle de St.-Pierre was decorated by writer, filmmaker, and painter Jean Cocteau, who spent part of his childhood here. Just beyond town is mansion-filled Cap-Ferrat and Beaulieu-sur-Mer, worth a stop for its down-to-the-details "Greek estate" built by a German archaeologist in the early 20th century.

   Coming up: high drama. The Moyenne Corniche offers views over cliff and sea. The medieval hilltop village of Èze offers even greater vistas. The cliff-topping Grand Corniche supersedes the Roman Via Aurelia. In the town of Turbie, you can't miss the Trophée des Alpes, the domineering monument denoting the 13 B.C. victory of Augustus over 44 Ligurian tribes. Jet-set-central Monaco caps off this stellar road trip.

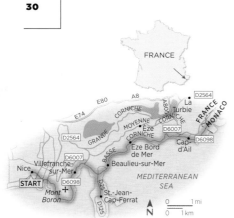

travelwise

Start Nice **End** Monaco **Distance** 21 miles (34 km)
Roads D6098, D6007, D2564—the three Corniche roads
Insider Tip In the town of Èze, challengingly steep shop-filled lanes climb to the Jardin Exotique, planted with hundreds of species of cacti and succulents amid old fortress ruins. The icing on the cake? Stupendous views.

amalfi charms

Switchback roads • Take-your-breath-away views • Colorful villages

Think twice about doing this drive in the busy months of July and August. And given the sometimes downright harrowing roads, it's not a bad idea to break up the trip with a couple of overnights along the way.

Leave Sorrento and pick up the spur to rugged Punta Campanella, a hiker's delight. The village of Sant'Agata sui Due Golfi, as its name suggests, commands views over two gulfs, those of Naples to the north and Salerno to the south.

After the popular town of Positano, you'll hit Vettica (known for its colorfully domed church) and Praiano, where the road turns really rugged. A short distance farther is the Grotta dello Smeraldo, or Emerald Grotto, accessible via elevator or steps. If there's time, follow the steep road through Furore (known for its wines; buy some for later) and onto the high plateau around Agerola.

Stretch out in the town of Amalfi or Ravello. Beyond, Capo d'Orso is a protected cape—one of the loveliest parts of the coast. Just before Vietri sul Mare, celebrated for its ceramics, you'll drive through Cetara, known for its tuna industry.

travelwise

Start Sorrento   **End** Vietri sul Mare   **Distance** 50 miles (80 km)
Roads Local roads, SS145, SS163
Inside Tip Positano may be touristy, but if you love linen, pay a visit. Many a shop sells locally made—and fairly priced—linen dresses and shirts.

The gardens of Villa Rufolo in Ravello (left). A Positano hallmark: stairs everywhere (right).

the garden route

Sandy beaches • Lucky elephants • Sporting options

A climb up the St. Blaise Lighthouse could reward with whale or dolphin spottings, though you are guaranteed fine visuals at the town museums. Moving on, the town of George is the center of South Africa's golf route as well as a hotbed of colonial buildings. Local flora takes center stage at the Garden Route Botanical Garden.

After you pass the no longer wild town of Wilderness, drive through Wilderness National Park, aflutter with birds that are drawn by lagoons and lakes. Just west of seaside Sedgefield is a Saturday market with fresh produce and local crafts.

On a pretty lagoon surrounded by forest, Knysna is a good place to stop for a bite to eat. Next up is something quite moving. The Knysna Elephant Park offers a 148-acre (60 ha) habitat for orphaned elephants who can safely roam free. Guides permit close contact with these marvelous animals. Farther east along the N2, the seaside village of Plettenberg Bay rubs elbows with miles and miles of beautiful beaches. Keep your eye on the surf for dolphins (summer) and whales (winter). At Storms River, sign up for adventure, from mountain biking to bungee jumping.

travelwise

Start Mossel Bay   **End** Storms River   **Distance** 121 miles (195 km)
Road N2 (the Garden Route)
Insider Tip Ride a horse along the sand and through the aqua surf at Buffalo Bay, a beach that draws surfers as well as equestrians.

Opposite: Scenic Mossel Bay is a popular stop along the Garden Route.   Below: An African elephant in Knysna Elephant Park

23

a chennai spin

Urban beaches • Stunning architecture • Thriving metropolis

Formerly called Madras, Chennai juxtaposes history and modernity. Visit San Thome Cathedral, housing relics of St. Thomas the Apostle, said to have come to India in A.D. 52. Kapaleeshwarar Temple is the place for busy bazaars. Kamaraj Road along the marina is notable for its Victorian buildings. Look for the circular 1842 former Vivekananda House, used to store blocks of ice imported from America. Nearby, the Presidency College, designed in part by Robert F. Chisholm, is known for mixing French and Italian Renaissance styles with local details.

Continuing on, note the Public Water Works, Chepauk Palace, and Chisholm's University Senate House. From Fort St. George head to St. Mary's Church, where Job Charnock, who would later found Calcutta, had his daughters baptized.

Have a look at the Indo-Saracenic High Courts before driving past the arcades of Chennai Central Station and St. Andrew's Kirk, considered India's most important church. Finally, see why the Government Museum Complex is called the Pantheon.

travelwise

Start San Thome Cathedral   **End** Government Museum Complex
Distance 4 miles (6.4 km)
Roads Local roads (it makes most sense to leave things to a pro and hire a driver)
Insider Tip The Connemara Hotel, not far from the museum, has an excellent lunch buffet of local dishes, served in the Verandah Coffee Shop.

A woman sells grilled corn along the beach in Chennai.

Limestone stacks called the Twelve Apostles rise from Victoria's dramatic southern coastline.

great ocean road

Melbourne metro pleasures • Fishing ports • Beach rock formations

Tool around Melbourne (shops, restaurants, culture) before heading to the Great Ocean Road—built as a monument to World War I soldiers.

A longtime vacation spot, Torquay and its prime beaches hit the surfer radar in the 1960s and the culture is still going strong.

At Anglesea, it's not unusual to see kangaroos grazing on the golf course. Beyond, along the beach-laced coast, you'll come to the picturesque, fashionable seaside town of Lorne. Climb a trail behind town to see Erskine Falls and grand ocean views. Around Apollo Bay, the curvy drive couples with spectacular views, making it tough to drive cautiously.

June into September (winter hereabouts), southern right whales swim the shallows off the old whaling town of Warrnambool, the end point of this spectacular drive.

travelwise

Start Melbourne **End** Warrnambool **Distance** 260 miles (418 km)
Roads Princess Freeway (M1), Great Ocean Road (B100)
Insider Tip Farm-produced Apostle Whey Cheese (10 varieties) is made not far from the Twelve Apostles; visit for free tastings and to see the cows being milked.

Sunset behind the Ruakokore Anglican church

coastal east cape

Traditional Maori towns •
Beckoning beaches • Natural
surroundings

The East Cape shows the least European
influence of any region on the North Island.
Outside Gisborne sits Whangarei, a picturesque Maori town whose bay served as
the set for the film *Whale Rider*.

Past stunning Tolaga Bay is Tikitiki
(notable for its church) and the small settlement of Te Araroa. In the schoolyard
grows a massive tree, 131 feet (40 m)
around.

Past Te Araroa, Hicks Bay has a great
beach. You'll skirt the coast before reaching Waihau Bay. Following this is 65 miles
(105 km) of glorious beach and bay scenery
—the best of the journey. At Raukokore,
the photogenic Anglican church stands
out on a lonely promontory. From here,
the road winds and dips through a string
of bays. Farther on the road winds spec-
tacularly along the Motu River. Get ready
for awe-inspiring views of mountain, river,
and sea. On the way to Opotiki—one of
the first places settled by Maori—you will
pass a number of tiny settlements and
lonely beaches.

travelwise

Start Gisborne **End** Opotiki
Distance 205 miles (330 km)
Roads SH35, local roads
Don't Miss Whangarei's finely carved
meetinghouse • The climb to the top of
the East Cape lighthouse; great views
await • A stroll through Raukokore

cities
and beyond

Bright lights and crowded bars capture the vibrant energy of Miami, Florida.

26

east from montreal

Urban appeal • Rich vineyards • Stunning scenic views

Start this magical loop in Francophone Montreal and allow at least five days for this embarrassment-of-riches drive. From Montreal, head east to Chambly, whose canal locks remain manually operated. Take to the Route des Vignobles and find out why this is a top wine region. Enjoy vistas of Lake Champlain, Vermont, and the Adirondacks along the way. On Route 245, detour to the beautifully situated Abbaye de Saint-Benoît-du-Lac. Farther on, walk through historic Sherbrooke, home to several good museums. For some time travel, visit Drummondville's re-created open-air village. Cross the St. Lawrence for a stroll through Trois-Rivières, Quebec's second oldest city. At the end of Highway 138, Canada's first viable road, hop the ferry to pretty Sorel and its old town market. Follow the Richelieu River to Mont-Saint-Hilaire—an enchanting artist colony—before returning to Montreal.

travelwise

Start Montreal **End** Montreal **Distance** 385 miles (620 km)
Roads Highway 10, Routes 223, 202, 245, Highways 112, 143, 132, 55, 138, 158, 133, 116; this route includes a ferry
Insider Tip In the Trois-Rivières area spend the night at Manoir Becancourt, a boutique hotel and spa.

A brightly painted mural in Sherbrooke, Quebec

The sunset paints an amber glow on the hoodoos—natural columns of rock—in Dinosaur Provincial Park.

a calgary circle

Big-city pleasures • Alpine scenery • Dinosaur lore

After you've enjoyed Calgary's rich assortment of museums make your way to the Bar U Ranch National Historic Site to learn about ranching. Farther on, the focus is mining at the Leitch Collieries, a good prelude to the nearby Bellevue Underground Mine, where you'll don a hard hat and descend.

The rolling Great Plains meet the Canadian Rockies at wildlife-filled Waterton Lakes National Park. Stretch your legs if you like. Drive past stunning Red Rock Canyon—pink rock cut by sapphire water—and descend the prairie hills to the Remington-Alberta Carriage Centre in Cardston, a celebration of horse-drawn conveyances—beautiful but not equipped for lengthy road trips.

Prehistoric people and bison are the focus at Head-Smashed-In Buffalo Jump; fossils are spotlighted at Dinosaur Provincial Park. Farther along, the Royal Tyrrell Museum of Paleontology is one of the world's top dinosaur museums.

travelwise

Start Calgary **End** Calgary **Distance** 750 miles (1,207 km)
Roads Highway 2, Route 543, Highways 22, 3, 6, 5, 4, 36, Trans-Canada 1, Highways 56, 9
Insider Tip The Prince of Wales Hotel in Waterton Lakes National Park is one of Canada's iconic hotels. Spend the night, or stop in for afternoon tea from 2 to 5 p.m.

New York City cabs and flashing lights breathe life into legendary Fifth Avenue.

down fifth avenue

World-class art • Dazzling shops • Iconic buildings

Fifth Avenue is the pulse of a world-class metropolis. Hop in a cab at the Metropolitan Museum of Art and have the driver head south along Central Park past the Plaza Hotel, Bergdorf Goodman, Tiffany, FAO Schwarz, and a parade of other household-name places.

Off to the right between 48th and 51st Streets is Rockefeller Center. To your left loom the Gothic spires of St. Patrick's Cathedral. At the corner of 45th, on the left, look up to see the multicolored art deco faience work on the Fred F. French Building. It's a national historic landmark, as is the Flatiron Building between 23rd and 22nd Streets, which when it was completed in 1902 was one of the city's tallest.

South of 23rd Street, the buildings are not as tall; the retail outlets, more edgy. As you approach Washington Square Park you might do a double take. The park's imposing arch is a dead ringer for the Arc de Triomphe in Paris.

travelwise

Start 82nd Street and Fifth Avenue   **End** Eighth Street and Fifth Avenue
Distance 4 miles (6.4 km)
Road Fifth Avenue, a one-way thoroughfare running north-south
Don't Miss Window displays at Bergdorf Goodman • Patience and Fortitude—the marble lions guarding the 42nd Street Library • The Empire State Building

miami to the keys

Art deco hotels • Jungle gardens • Hemingway heritage

After a deco-hotels-district drive and a stop at the regal Italian Renaissance villa called Vizcaya, leave the city and make your way to Fairchild Tropical Botanic Garden, 83 acres (33.5 ha) of lily ponds and lush plantings. Nearby Parrot Jungle and Gardens, a 1930s tourist mecca, has flamingos, tortoises, and monkeys.

Blue-green water makes up the bulk of Biscayne National Park, an aquatic paradise that's home to marine life, viewable via glass-bottom-boat and snorkel excursions.

Drop by the visitor center to get the skinny on 1.5-million-acre (607,000 ha) Everglades National Park, where turtles, alligators, and crocodiles run free. Continuing south you'll cross 42 Keys-straddling bridges en route to Key West. On the way, enjoy the hibiscus and palms edging the road, snorkel at the National Marine Sanctuary on Key Largo, and take five at Bahia Honda State Park's sandy beach.

In Key West, it's all about good times, Hemingway's house, and conch fritters. Kick back; enjoy.

travelwise

Start Miami **End** Key West **Distance** 240 miles (386 km)
Roads U.S. 41/Florida A1A, Florida 9336, U.S. 1 Overseas Highway, local roads
Insider Tip Key Largo's John Pennekamp Coral Reef State Park—the nation's first underwater park—provides habitat for more than 600 species of fish and 40 kinds of coral. It's probably the best place in the U.S. to learn how to scuba dive.

Seven Mile Bridge cuts through Pigeon Key (left). The art deco exterior of Miami's South Seas Hotel (right).

sunset boulevard

Stunning strolls • Unforgettable characters • True glitz

Heading east on Sunset from Pacific Palisades, start out spiritually (so California) at the Self-Realization Fellowship Lake Shrine, which underscores the highly ecumenical nature of L.A. Hinduism and offers a meditative environment.

A left turn on Bienveneda takes you to the Topanga Trailhead and some mighty fine hiking through the Santa Monica Mountains. The Phil Leacock Memorial Trail comes with views of the Pacific Palisades and the Pacific Ocean. Back on Sunset, pause at Gelson's, the local favorite supermarket—part of an iconic California chain—where there's Wi-Fi (free), sushi made fresh daily, and loads of road trip snackables. Stop and nosh at nearby Will Rogers State Historic Park. The well-loved humorist deeded his estate to the state of California, which continues to maintain his home—and polo field. In the park is Inspiration Trail, nice to hike in the late afternoon when the fog rolls in.

Crossing Sunset, continue to Bel Air Estates. Either of the two entrances on the north side of Sunset offer admittance to the warren of small streets lined with some of the city's priciest homes, many offering proof that money and good taste don't always go hand in hand. Don't put much trust in the "star maps" hawked hereabouts; they are generally fictitious.

Celeb-spotting in Beverly Hills drops the curtain on an appropriate note. Practice the sport on the street (where even the fanciest shops sometimes have sales) or at the Beverly Hills Hotel's Polo Lounge, a haunt for Hollywood dealmakers.

travelwise

Start Pacific Palisades **End** Beverly Hills **Distance** 20 miles (32 km)
Roads Sunset Boulevard, Bienveneda Avenue
Insider Tip The Whisky A Go-Go (8901 Sunset), a rock history pantheon, has present-day cred—funky nightclub with a good sound system and cool groups.

Opposite: Palm trees line the boulevards of Beverly Hills.   Below: Mount Lee's iconic Hollywood sign

azuero experience

Colonial villages • Charming crafts • Wildlife (including iguanas!)

A drive through the southeast wedge of Panama's fat finger of land called Azuero feels like a trip back in time. Countryside intermingles with unspoiled villages, and a national park is imbued with a sense of forever. Start by turning south at Dívisa, soon diverting north to the austere Sarigua National Park, Panama's most important pre-Columbian site. Continuing south, stop for a stroll along Parita's quaint cobblestone streets. In the tidy village of La Arena, shop for ceramics.

The town of Chitré is worth a stop for its museum and cathedral. Similar cultural pleasures await in Las Tablas. For the final 26 miles (42 km) of the trip to the sleepy town of Pedasí, the settlements are less prosperous; creaky horse-drawn carts the transportation norm. In contrast, the wildlife on Isla Iguana and at the Cañas Wildlife Reserve is bountiful. The trip concludes with exquisite mountain scenery and Pacific Ocean views.

travelwise

Start The Inter-American Highway near Divisa   **End** Pedasí
Distance 70 miles (113 km)
Roads Inter-American Highway, Carretera Nacional (National Highway), local roads
Insider Tip Roughly a 30-minute drive south from Pedasí, the beachside Villa Marina Retreat—a 9-room boutique property—is a good place to unwind for a couple of days.

Elaborate floats and costumes accentuate the festivities of a Carnival celebration in Panama.

A natural oasis in Peru is a welcome change from the surrounding barren desert.

pan-am highway

Beachside villages • Vineyard lands • Abundant wildlife

Beyond Peru's capital, detour at San Vicente de Cañete to visit the fishing hamlet of Cerro Azul, site of pre-Inca structures and present-day surfers. Midway between Chincha Alta (interesting for its Afro-Peruvian culture) and Ica (where Peru's best grapes grow) is the city of Pisco (famous for its namesake liquor).

South of Pisco, boat tours around the Ballestas Islands get you close to pods of sea lions. Back on land you will find the fascinating Nasca Lines, dating back some 2,000 years. These huge pictures are best seen from above; local tour operators offer scenic flights.

Farther on, the road hugs the Pacific before heading inland to Moquegua, an agricultural center. The namesake town is worth a visit for its architecture and wood-fired pizza at the cowboy-themed El Bandido bar, open after 6 p.m. The route ends in anticlimactic Tacna—30 miles (48 km) from the Chilean border.

travelwise

Start Lima   **End** Tacna   **Distance** 827 miles (1,331 km)
Road Pan-American Highway South (Route 1)
Insider Tip Spend the night in Pisco, enjoying the famous liquor and scenic surroundings. The Hotel Majoro, a former monastery, is now a lovely oasis in the desert where you can relax by the pool and dine on authentic Peruvian cuisine.

ARGENTINA

33

along the salta loop

Red-rock canyons • Local crafts
• Snow-kissed peaks

Set aside at least three days for this counterclockwise odyssey through Argentina's
wild northwest. Your start top point,
Salta—one of South America's best
kept secrets—deserves a day or two
on its own.

About two hours into the trip, the road
starts its climb into the Quebrada de las
Conchas, where the river and its tributaries
have carved dramatic canyons. Cafayate,
in wine country, offers colonial ambience
coupled with good restaurants.

You might want to detour to Quilmes to
hike through cactus-studded ruins before
pressing on to Cachi, with an 18th-century
church, archaeological museum, and
superb mountain views. It's all about high-
altitude cactus at the Parque Nacional
Los Cardones. The stretch back to Salta
includes an awesomely steep descent.

travelwise

Start Salta **End** Salta
Distance 380 miles (612 km)
Roads RN 68, RN 40, RP 33
Insider Tip Savor Salta's street-food
turnovers at Patio de la Empanada; for
the best cheap eats in town, explore
(using your eyes and nose) the outdoor
Mercado Central food market.

High-altitude cacti are nestled in the foothills of mountains near Cachi

A multicolored flower bed in the Keukenhof gardens forms a river of color.

the tulip route

Bulbs in bloom • Tulip museum • Seaside towns

From late January through late July, it's all about bulbs. First stop is Lisse, an attractive town in the middle of a grand bulb-growing district. The small Museum de Zwarte Tulp celebrates the tulip's history—centuries ago, small fortunes were paid for prize bulbs. Just north of town, Keukenhof is planted to the hilt. Amid the riot of color are sculptures, pavilions serving as art galleries, and mazes.

Beyond the gardens, head through the bulb fields to Sassenheim. On the western edge of town is the pretty Kasteel Teilingen, an 11th-century castle. Nearby, Noordwijk aan Zee is a glorious sandy beach. In the city of Haarlem, before you head back toward Amsterdam, visit the Frans Hals Museum. Zandvoort, the beach closest to Amsterdam, can be awfully busy in summer, but behind the strip of beach is the quiet National Park de Kennemerduinen, which attracts many rare and unusual birds, including black-tailed godwits and sand reed buntings.

travelwise

Start Amsterdam **End** Amsterdam **Distance** 61 miles (98 km)
Roads Vijzelstraat, S100, S106, A10/E22, A4/E19, N207, N208, N443, N206, A9
Insider Tip Pancakes—savory as well as sweet—are a culinary staple in the Netherlands. A good place to eat as the locals do is the Pannenkoeken Brasserie Vrouw Holle, right near the Keukenhof gardens.

old world cities

35 London by Bus, England

Buckingham Palace? St. Paul's Cathedral? London Eye? Board a coach (Brit for bus), sit back, and let someone else do the on-the-left driving. Yes, London's famous red double-decker (known as the Routemaster) was mothballed in 2005 (largely due to old age), but there's a new and improved version whose debut was planned to coincide with the 2012 Olympics. It is hybrid diesel-electric with an interior reminiscent of a sleek hotel lobby. More good news: The fun "hop on, hop off" option remains.
www.tfl.gov.uk

36 Glasgow to St. Andrews, Central Belt, Scotland

The 95-mile (153 km) west–east route takes in three castles (Stirling, Campbell, St. Andrews), one extremely grand but incomplete residence (16th-century Mar's Wark), a string of towns, beautiful Dollar Glen, and, finally, the home of golf. On foot: An under-4-hour stroll around the city of Stirling includes some of Scotland's most famous historic and cultural sites.
www.visitscotland.com

37 Out of Athens, Attica, Greece

A 120-mile (193 km) drive starting at the Greek capital and winding up in Halkida serves as a Greece-in-miniature experience. It's a route of high hills, beaches, small villages, old churches, and classical sights. Musts: the awe-inspiring Temple of Poseidon (ca 440 B.C.) and a stop for some authentic Greek food (vegetarians fare particularly well).
www.athensguide.org/attica

38 Bosporus Tour, Turkey

Forget about driving through confusing, traffic-mad Istanbul. Most of the city's major sites are right on the water anyway, so a leisurely, hands-free taste of the metropolis that straddles two continents makes good sense. You'll boat past palaces, mosques, fortresses, waterside promenades. Best bet: a sunset cruise.
www.istanbul.com

Experience the sights of London on iconic Route 15.

moscow's golden ring

Cities large and small • Classic landmarks • Timeless beauty spots

Here's a loop journey—best enjoyed by going counterclockwise—that goes a long way to help travelers understand modern Russia. Tucked among groves, hills, and lakes—and enshrined in local folklore—are picturesque forts (called kremlins!), monasteries, and photo-op gold-dome churches. The capital of Russia in the 12th century, Vladimir retains a charmingly provincial air amid a wealth of monasteries, museums, and churches. Before building nearly half of Moscow's Kremlin, Italian architect Aristotle Fioravanti studied the architecture of Vladimir's must-see 12th-century Assumption Cathedral. A highlight of the drive, the hilly town of Suzdal is a green dream: The old architecture and buildings are officially protected.

Situated on the Volga River, Kostroma is great for a stroll. Shops and markets fill 18th-century riverside arcades. Rostov-Velikiy is a city of pleasing architecture and design. The neoclassical interior of the green-domed Yakovlevsky Monastery is a colorful surprise. Pereslavl'-Zalessky, basically a one-street town, is one of central Russia's most ancient cities. Just to the east of town, the Danilovsky Monastery and Trinity Cathedral is a 16th-century treat. Before heading back to Moscow, visit unusual Kukushka, a "museum" of defunct narrow-gauge rail cars.

travelwise

Start Moscow   **End** Moscow   **Distance** 420 miles (676 km)
Roads Local roads
Insider Tip The easiest way to travel the Golden Ring is to hire a guide in Moscow to accompany you along the sometimes challenging route. He or she can help you follow the road signs, many of which aren't in English.

Opposite: Ilya Prorok's (Elijah the Prophet) ornate interior   Below: St. Demetrius Byzantine church, Vladimir

40

a west bank loop

Temples galore • King Tut's tomb • The legendary Nile

The road to the ancient monuments runs almost perfectly straight through canal-irrigated fields. The first attention getters are the mud structures of New Gurna, a model village designed in 1946. Next up is your first West Bank monument spotting, the Colossi of Memnon, a lone pair of towering statues standing in a field. More monumental is the Ramesseum, a mortuary tribute to a powerful pharaoh. Huddled on the slopes to the left are the colorful houses of Old Gurna.

Moving on, turn left at the T-junction. You'll pass the domed Howard Carter's House, where the noted Egyptologist lived during his search for an unrobbed tomb. He hit what just might be the mother lode: Tutankhamun's riches-filled final resting place. The final gem of the route is the Valley of the Kings, a trove of dozens of 16th- to 11th-century B.C. tombs.

travelwise

Start West Bank ferry landing   **End** West Bank ferry landing
Distance 12 miles (19 km)
Roads Local roads
Insider Tip This route, most expediently experienced via taxi, also can be enjoyed by bike or even on foot.

Majestic and awe inspiring, a sphinx at the Luxor Temple reflects a golden hue.

Cascades near Sefrou (left). A woman walks with sheep, with the snowy Atlas Mountains looming in the background (right).

beyond fès

Spring-fed valleys • High terrain and gorges • Fabulous mountain views

After leaving Fès make sure to slow down through the province of Sefrou, whose spectacular scenery centers on its waterfalls. The capital of the province—named Sefrou, too—is a river town surrounded by huge 18th-century ramparts. Stroll the old part of town, dominated by the Grand Mosque, north of the river.

As you head south, the weather turns much cooler, thanks to the extreme change in altitude. You'll find small Berber settlements on the way to the market town of Midelt, a popular starting point for summer treks—not for newbies—into the mountains. The area is characterized by dramatic gorges. The road beyond Midelt follows a tortuous course as it heads higher into the High Atlas Mountains before descending into the gorgeous Ziz Valley. Pass through the small, marvelously named village of Rich and dune-swept Merzouga. At the end of the drive, at the edge of the Sahara is the 20th-century French town of Er Rachidia.

travelwise

Start Fès   **End** Er Rachidia   **Distance** 212 miles (341 km)
Roads N8, N 13
Insider Tip Sefrou's countryside is awash in cherry trees. The week-long annual Cherry Festival in mid-June, celebrated since 1920, coincides with the cherry harvest.

OMAN

42
along a mideast coast

Shipyards • Turtles • Souks

Oman is blessed with Arabian Sea coast-line—and enticing white-sand beaches. After seeing the capital city's sights, you'll head south, crossing the Hajar Mountains, whose slopes plunge into the sea. Along the road, goats and their herders, white-washed villages, and rock formations show Oman in a timeless light.

Must-stop spots are the harbor town of Quriyat (with coastal plain views) and the village of Dibab (Dibab Lake Park's sinkhole is filled with remarkably clear blue water—wonderful for swimming). Two more tempting take-a-dip spots are palm-shaded Wadi Shab and Fins Beach, one of Oman's most beautiful meetings of sand and sea.

Before Sur, pause in the ancient city of Qalhat for a look at the Bibi Maryam mausoleum, thought to be a remnant of a mosque deemed one of the most beautiful in the world by a 12th-century explorer. A placid sea town, Sur was for centuries a leading trading post; it remains a place of twisty streets and fine old houses. Learn about dhow trading ships at Sur's Maritime Museum.

travelwise

Start Muscat   **End** Sur
Distance 149 miles (240 km)
Roads Al-Amirate Road and Route 17
Don't Miss Enormous Sultan Qaboos Grand Mosque • During low tide, a walk to the watchtower-topped island off Quriyat • The Ras al-Hadd Turtle Reserve

Lit up against the night sky, the Sultan Qaboos Grand Mosque near Muscat can accommodate 20,000 worshippers.

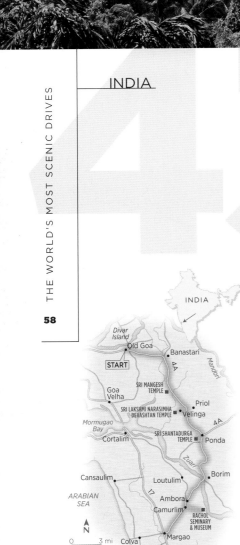

Gazing over the tops of green trees stand majestic churches in Old Goa.

INDIA

discovering goa

Hindu temples • Pieces of Portugal past • Covered markets

The capital of Portugal's Indian empire until 1843, Old Goa rewards today's travelers with museums, historic buildings, temples and churches, great food, and a vibrant nightlife. But back to worship for a moment.

Beyond the city, in a secluded valley, are the temples of Ponda—places of refuge for Hindu priests fleeing Portuguese missionaries in the 18th century. Nearby are three major Buddhist temples. Perhaps the most beautiful is Sri Lakshmi Narashimha Devashtan, in the idyllic woodlands of Velinga.

Shortly after the road crosses the Zuari River you'll come to the town of Margao, whose one-way streets are lined with grand old houses. Do go inside the gleaming white Church of the Holy Spirit to see the baroque and rococo details. Margao's busy covered market is where the locals stock up on spices, vegetables, and the other ingredients that make the regional fare so very tasty.

travelwise

Start Old Goa   **End** Margao   **Distance** 20 miles (32 km)
Roads NH4A and local roads
Insider Tip In tiny Ambora, between Ponda and Margao, you'll find a loved-by-locals sweets spot: Jila Bakery turns out must-taste cookies; Indira Gandhi was a fan.

phnom penh ride

Sights uniquely witnessed • Lively markets • Mischievous monkeys

Given the traffic and absence of sidewalks, the city is best experienced in a breezy, slow-moving fashion—via *tuk-tuk*, a motorbike hitched to an open-air cabin. Sit back and enjoy as someone else handles the driving!

You'll head west past Hun Sen Park with its statues of Khmer literary figures and continue to Independence Monument. Continue on to the Royal Palace and Silver Pagoda (the royal family's residence), ornate Wat Ounalom, art deco Central Market, and the riverfront—lined with shops and restaurants.

Back on the road, look skyward to catch a glimpse of Wat Phnom's soaring pagoda. At peaceful Wat Lanka, Buddhist monks provide meditation instruction on some evenings. Moving 180 degrees on the emotional scale, the Tuol Sleng Genocide Museum was once the notorious S-21 Khmer Rouge detention center.

You wind up at the Russian Market, where, rather than nesting dolls, the goods range from custom-made clothing to easy-to-pack souvenirs.

travelwise

Start Vietnamese Friendship Monument   **End** Russian Market
Distance 2 miles (3 km)
Roads Local streets
Don't Miss Norodom Boulevard's colonial villas • Wat Phnom and its mischievous monkeys • The Russian Market's popular-brand clothing, local crafts, and silk robes

A tuk-tuk waits outside the Royal Palace in Phnom Penh.

AUSTRALIA

the pacific highway

Rain forests • Surfing beaches • Koalas

Like today's Route 66 (rather than the fabled stretch of endless Americana) the Pacific Highway can be heavily trafficked, potholed, and not all that diverting. That's the bad news. But the good news more than compensates, starting with the city of Newcastle's heritage buildings, thriving arts and food scenes, and good beaches. From Newcastle you can detour west (to the famed Hunter Valley wine region or the rain forests of Barrington Tops National Park) or continue northeast, keeping an eye out for koalas in the bush around Lemon Tree Passage. The nearby Koala Hospital, with some 200 injured and sick koalas, is open to visitors.

Tucked in the rain forest, laid-back Bellingen is a magnet for creative types. Drive up the Route 78 escarpment to the rain forests of Dorrigo National Park. At Coffs Harbour sits a piece of memorable roadside kitsch, the Big Banana.

You'll end in Byron Bay, one of the prettiest spots on the coast. This popular resort is filled with vegetarian cafés, organic markets, art galleries, and folk music.

travelwise

Start Sydney   **End** Byron Bay   **Distance** 520 miles (837 km)
Roads Routes 1, 15, 78
Insider Tip The village of Nimbin—45 miles (72 km) west of Byron Bay—is a 1970s time warp of dreadlocks, bare feet, psychedelia, spiritual healers, and tie-dye. Kick back with a cup of organic coffee at one of the hip cafés.

Opposite: A koala snuggles on a branch in an Australian sanctuary.   Below: Byron Bay surfers share a wave.

backr
rambles

oad

A classic New England church is the heart of a small village in Vermont.

Two ice climbers carefully traverse Columbia Icefield in Jasper National Park.

CANADA

icefields parkway

World-class national parks • Grand-dame hotels • Views, views, views

The two-lane Icefields Parkway sets the stage for one of the world's most scenic road trips. Driving northwest through the Rockies you start off in Canada's original national park, Banff National Park (and adjoining Jasper National Park). Take in a vast tangle of imposing peaks, capped with the largest ice fields south of Alaska. Prowling the wilds are cougars, coyote, caribou, bears, and more.

At Johnston Canyon, a narrow limestone chasm 11 miles (18 km) northwest of Banff, take an under-2-mile (3 km) hike through waterfall country. The trail is usually crowded but not nearly as populated as the nearby shores of Lake Louise.

The "oh wow" views keep on coming as you head toward Jasper. But don't rush to the finish line. Just beyond powerful Athabasca Falls take the 9-mile (14 km) side trip to Mount Edith Cavell, a vast wall of rock and snow that sweeps upward nearly a vertical mile (half a km) from the parking area.

travelwise

Start Banff **End** Jasper **Distance** 186 miles (300 km)
Roads Icefields Parkway/Highway 93, local roads
Don't Miss The cave and hot springs at Cave and Basin National Historic Site, a Banff highlight • A look—or overnight—at Banff Springs Hotel and/or Chateau Lake Louise • Icefield Centre, a thronged activity and education hub in Jasper National Park

newfoundland fun

Old European settlements • A wealth of wildlife • Moody seascapes

Roaming caribou and the odd roadside moose dot the landscape, though the life you'll find in St. John's has more to do with creative verve. The arts thrive here.

Signal Hill's fortifications date back to the days of Napoleon. A ferry at Bay Bulls takes you to the islands that make up Witless Bay Ecological Reserve (seabirds galore). Back on the mainland, stop at Ferryland, an early English settlement. Looping south you'll see vast seascapes sometimes cloaked in fog. Beyond St. Vincent's watch for whales. Head north to Brigus, an enchanting village easily explored by a self-guided walking tour.

Beyond the historic Heart's Content Cable Station, Heart's Desire, and Heart's Delight, Trinity is a not-to-be-missed gem. Settled in 1501, it retains a timeless stage-set ambience. Just before Bonavista, the road crests, offering a fabulous view of this 500-year-old seaport, its buildings looking like little toys dropped every which way.

travelwise

Start St. John's **End** Bonavista **Distance** 430 miles (692 km)
Roads Highways 10, 90, 70, 74, 80, 230, Trans-Canada 1, local roads
Insider Tip George Street in St. John's is pub and bar central. You'll find more than 20 such establishments, many offering live entertainment. O'Reilly's is the place for traditional Celtic music.

Waterfront in Brigus Harbour, a quaint Newfoundland village

48

riding vermont 100

Year-round splendor • Inviting villages • Sweet mountain scenery

The Main Street of the state's Green Mountains, Vermont 100 runs through typical Yankee heartland. Early into the trip, with the Deerfield River on your right and Haystack Mountain on your left, the road climbs to the lofty village of West Dover and cuts through Green Mountain National Forest.

Continue north to Weston, known for its playhouse and the famous Vermont Country Store, purveyors of goods that reflect strong Yankee values. From here the ride flirts with hills en route to Ludlow, a factory town that's been gentrified with shops and restaurants. The road then takes you along lakes and rivers to Calvin Coolidge country; it was in tiny Plymouth Notch that he was sworn in as president in August 1923.

Beyond ski-worthy Stowe and on the way to Newport—near the Canadian border—the mountains give way to broad vistas.

travelwise

Start Wilmington **End** Newport **Distance** 188 miles (303 km)
Road Vermont 100
Don't Miss President Calvin Coolidge State Historic Site and nearby Plymouth Cheese Factory (founded by the President's dad) • The Ben & Jerry's factory, just beyond the village of Waterbury • The charming village of Weston

Painted red, the Weston Old Mill Museum gives a rustic feel that transports one back in time.

Rare double waterfalls join to form Smith Creek in northern Georgia.

chattahoochee!

A river wild • Georgia's high point • Blue Ridge country

Drive through Chattahoochee National Forest, with trees, valleys, mountains, and a rushing river for company. At Robertstown, a 3-mile (5 km) detour lands you at Unicoi State Park, whose crown jewel is Anna Ruby Falls. Back on the main route, the road gets steeper as it approaches Brasstown Bald (4,784 feet, 1,458 m), named for its treeless summit.

Continue on through exquisite Blue Ridge landscapes and get onto Richard Russell Scenic Byway, which parallels the Nottely River. Before returning to Helen, stop at Dukes Creek Falls and take the short trail to the observation tower to get an idea of where you've just been.

travelwise

Start Helen   **End** Helen   **Distance** 41 miles (66 km)
Roads Georgia 17/75, 356, 180, 348, Richard Russell Scenic Byway, 75 Alternate
Insider Tip A good way to experience the Chattahoochee River is atop a horse. In summer, the trail horses actually walk right through the 'Hooch (you stay high and dry).

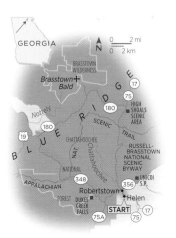

route 66

50

Vintage diners and motels • A slice of Grand Canyon
• Volcanic formations

A veritable household name venerated in story and song, Route 66 is a shadow
of its former self, largely superseded by newer roads. You can, however, still drive
along sections of the original. Head out west toward Tucumcari, a town that takes
its Route 66 heritage to heart—its signs have been restored to their 1950s dazzle.

Farther west, highlights include the Las Vegas National Wildlife Refuge, Pecos
National Historic Park, and stupendous Santa Fe. Past Albuquerque, the town of
Grants is the gateway to El Malpais National Monument, a badlands of lava flows,
cinder cones, and other volcanic formations. Be sure to take the side trip to
Petrified Forest National Park, where petrified logs dating from 225 million years
ago prompt double takes. The Blue Mesa and Long Logs Trails reward brief hikes
with stunning landscapes. From Holbrook, good side trips include the kitschy
Wigwam Motel and the Meteor Crater, which immortalizes the power of a meteor,
equivalent to 20 million tons of TNT.

Flagstaff is the southern gateway to the Grand Canyon, while the railroad town
of Seligman is the first of several towns awash in 1950s trappings, from drive-ins
to shops. At the end of the route, desert gives way to the Colorado River.

travelwise

Start Glenrio, New Mexico **End** Topock, Arizona
Distance 733 miles (1,180 km)
Roads I-40, New Mexico 333, 122, 118, U.S. 180/Historic Route 66
Insider Tip At Mr. D'z's diner in Kingman, chow down on baby back ribs or
a vegetarian sandwich, but make sure the chaser is their famous root beer.

Opposite: Neon lights of the Galaxy Diner   Below: An old-model car rests outside a tepee motel in Holbrook.

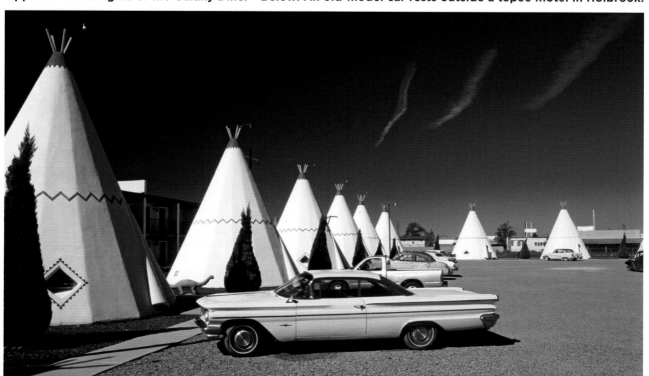

Water pours from the "weeping wall" along Going-to-the-Sun Road.

MONTANA

to-the-sun road

Lush forest • Ribbon-like waterfalls • Wildflower meadows

Crossing Glacier National Park's eastern spine via this spectacular road comes with a wealth of "oh wows." At Wild Goose Lake turnout you'll see a tiny mountain-dwarfed island; some 5 miles (8 km) beyond, a trail leads to St. Mary Falls, an exquisite cascade. The next stretch—through forest—is home to red squirrels, black bears, great horned owls, and other fauna. Grizzly bears, bighorn sheep, and mountain goats can often be spotted farther on.

En route to 6,646-foot (2,025 m) Logan Pass, the park's expansive mountain ranges come into full view. Beyond the pass, a knife-edged crest that runs down the Continental Divide separates the Atlantic and Pacific watersheds. Stop at Bird Woman Falls overlook to admire the mountain-framed waterfalls.

Before you come to Apgar, take a walk along one of the broad pebble beaches lining Lake McDonald—an imposing 10 miles (16 km) long.

travelwise

Start St. Mary   **End** Apgar   **Distance** 50 miles (80 km)
Roads Going-to-the-Sun Road (Route 89)
Insider Tip: To navigate this engineering feat of a road—and get through its tunnels—your vehicle must be no longer than 21 feet (6.4 m), wider than 8 feet (2.4 m), or higher than 10 feet (3 m).

death valley drive

Profound heat • Canyons of marble • Sere lowlands

When it comes to "civilization" in one of the world's greatest desert realms, it's all about the road. This drive begins in nondescript Olancha, the place to buy gas, water, and snacks. Head east, and shortly after skirting Owens Lake Bed (dry as a bone), you'll enter Death Valley National Park. As you motor into the Panamint Range, keep an eye out for Aguereberry Point, at 6,433 feet (1,961 m).

Back on the highway, you'll pass the tiny resort of Stovepipe Wells. A side trip leads to the mouth of Mosaic Canyon and a short walk through a water-carved marble landscape. Farther along, another side trip delivers you to Scotty's Castle (a Mediterranean-style mansion). Around Furnace Creek natural springs support flora, places to overnight, and even a golf course (very challenging).

Not far from the lowest spot in the hemisphere is Badwater (279 feet, 85 m below sea level), with pools saltier than the ocean. Toward the end of the route, take a side trip to Dantes View, where alluvial fans and salt flats sprawl below you.

travelwise

Start Olancha   **End** Death Valley Junction   **Distance** 130 miles (209 km)
Roads California 90, Badwater Road, local side roads
Insider tip: Death Valley is all about exploration. As you tool around, you might come upon ruins, hidden springs, chuckwalla lizards, kangaroo rats, even wild horses.

A small bush among the hardpan sand dunes in Death Valley

ALASKA

Opposite: Magnificent northern lights and a full moon shine brightly over the Turnagain Arm of Cook Inlet. Above: Sea lions relax and sun themselves on cool rocks.

seward highway

Visual overload • Dramatic bore tides • No-nonsense wildlife

An Alaska sampler—fjords, glaciers, mountains, lakes, evergreen forests, and wildlife-rich wetlands are in abundant supply. Head southwest out of Anchorage. Pause at the Anchorage Coastal Wildlife Refuge and look around. To the west across Cook Inlet is 11,070-foot (3,374 m) Mount Spurr; easterly views are dominated by the jagged ridges of the even taller Chugach Mountains. South, across Turnagain Arm, the spires of the Kenai Mountains crown the spruce and hemlock wilderness of Chugach National Forest.

Along Turnagain's north shore, the tides are grand—best witnessed from turnouts between miles 95 and 90 (km 153 and 145). Don't venture onto the flats; the quicksand can be deadly. Portage Lake is edged by gravel, perfect for a stroll.

At mile 37 (km 59.5) bear left for Seward. Nearby Tern Lake is a noted birdwatching site. Close by Moose Pass is a spunky hamlet. Near mile 4 (km 6.4), a good 9-mile (14.5 km) road leads to Exit Glacier in Kenai Fjords National Park.

travelwise

Start Anchorage   **End** Seward   **Distance** 127 miles (204 km)
Roads Seward Highway, blazed with mile markers
Insider Tip The sprawling, nonprofit Alaska Wildlife Conservation Center (mile 79; km 127) provides spacious sanctuary for injured and orphaned animals, from bears to bison, elk to owls. Human visitors welcome.

east end drive

Lonely bays • A truly stellar valley • Classic Hawaii

On the outskirts of town, heading east, you'll see Kalokoeli, one of dozens of centuries-old fishponds scalloping the shoreline. A few miles on, at Nene O Molokai, the endangered state bird (yes, the nene) is being raised for release into the wild. Tours, by appointment, are free.

Just past mile 10 (km 16), at the compact, white St. Joseph's Catholic Church, the Damien statue is always decked with fresh flowers. Farther down the road is the red-roof Our Lady of Seven Sorrows Catholic Church, built by Father Damien. On the National Register of Historic Places, 13th-century Iliiliopae is the island's oldest temple.

As the trip draws to an end, the road climbs inland then hairpins back to the sea for one of Hawaii's best views: Halawa Valley, with its dark sands, waterfalls, and frequent rainbows.

travelwise

Start Kaunakakai, Molokai **End** Halawa Valley **Distance** 27 miles (43 km)
Road Highway 450 (East End Drive)
Insider Tip In true Hawaii holiday spirit, each year from mid-December to mid-April some 10,000 humpback whales show up from Alaska to mate, give birth, and, well, just hang out.

The green-cloaked mountainside is a vision of undiluted Hawaiian solitude.

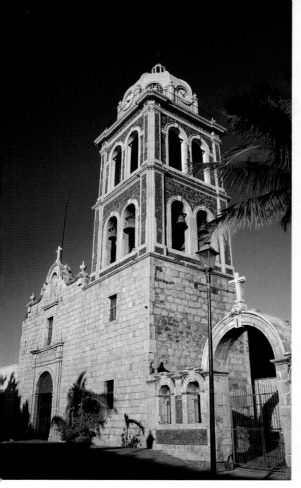

The ancient Mission of Loreto in Baja California (left). Bright green fish swim among the 20,000-year-old coral reef in Cabo Pulmo National Park (right).

baja expedition

Cactuses, canyons, coves • Ocean magic • Happenin' grand finale

This is one big trip. You can do the north–south route in four days but spending a week or more is the ticket. Leave early morning and break for a swim and lunch in San Quintín. Well along, Laguna Ojo de Liebre is a mating and birthing ground for gray whales and the site of a sizable salt-evaporation plant.

About halfway into the trip, you can stroll through the town of San Ignacio or hike its wild environs. A riverbed thick with lush palms marks the entrance to Mulegé, where keeping your eyes on the road becomes a real challenge. Take time out for a swim at Coyote Beach. About a 2-hour drive from here is Loreto; a 1-hour dirt-road side trip leads to Misión San Javier, an impressive historic church. Sailboarding is popular at Bahía de las Palmas; fishing and diving are the lures at Cabo Pulmo.

After this awe-inspiring adventure, the creature comforts of Cabo San Lucas are your just reward.

travelwise

Start Tijuana   **End** Cabo San Lucas   **Distance** 1,125 miles (1,811 km)
Road Highway 1
Don't Miss San Ignacio, a bona fide high-desert oasis • Bahía de la Concepción's clear aquamarine water, which appears like a glistening mirage • Fishing and diving at Cabo Pulmo, an underwater reserve

Investigating its surroundings, a resplendent quetzal looks out of its nest in Costa Rica.

56

caribbean wild

Scenic overload • Birds everywhere
• Hiking, fishing, horseback riding

This route along Costa Rica's mountain ridges positions you to see some of the most spectacular vistas in the country. Avoid the rainy season, May-November, when clouds compromise the views.

Cartago, former capital of Costa Rica, manages to be both modern and quaint. Within 15 minutes of leaving Cartago, be ready to climb winding roads. At Vara de Roble, the views down the mountain are sublime, but better still at Empalme (your last chance to buy gas). Orchards cling to forested slopes. Roadside trout farms offer fishing and horseback rides. Atop the crest of the Continental Divide you'll see the yellow church of Cañón.

Settlements thin as you drive through the Reserva Forestal Río Macho and the Iyöla Arnia Cloud Reserve. Near the 80 km (mile 50) marker a side road spirals sharply west. The hamlet of San Gerardo de Dota sits in a valley rich with orchards favored by quetzals. These birds are the focus at the Savegre Biological Reserve. On the way to Las Torres, the final highlight is the 11,450-foot (3,490 m) Cerro de la Muerte.

travelwise

Start Cartago   **End** Las Torres
Distance 45 miles (62 km)
Road Highway 2
Insider Tip Outside the modernist Dantica Cloud Forest Lodge and Gallery you can take a short hike in Parque Nacional Los Quetzales.

Farm lands zigzag along headland cliffs on the west end of Country Kerry.

the ring of kerry

Shaggy dunes • Bronze Age forts • Green, green, green

Head out at the break of day to get a jump on the traffic along Ireland's best known scenic route. Heading counterclockwise, the fine views begin on the outskirts of Killarney en route to the small town of Killorglin.

At the edge of Glenbeigh Village, turn right for Rossbehy Strand's wonderful view of a giant spit with miles of dunes stretching across Dingle Bay. Not quite halfway into the trip, follow the brown "Stone Houses" signs to find the perched Cahergal and Leacanabuaile forts, relics of the Bronze Age. A delightful spot of land with a patchwork of fields, cliffs, and subtropical gardens, Valentia Island sits across a causeway. Toward the end of the loop, climb the stone steps of the Staigue Fort—a holdout from 1500 B.C.—and be rewarded with sea and mountain views.

travelwise

Start Killarney **End** Killarney **Distance** 150 miles (241 km)
Roads N72, N70, local roads
Don't Miss Killorglin's August 10–12 Puck Festival, when a wild mountain goat is crowned "King Puck" • The needle-towered rocks Great Skellig and Little Skellig, sanctuaries for seabirds • A stroll from Derrynane House—former home of local hero Daniel O'Connell—to Mass Rock, a secret site of Catholic prayer in the 18th century

a cotswolds loop

Sweet towns • Pastures edged in stone • Grand arboretum

The sojourn begins and ends in Cheltenham, a classic spa town with impressive Regency architecture. Head southwest to quaint Painswick, a ridgetop village with a celebrated churchyard filled with ornate 18th-century tombs and dozens of yews.

A left turn 4 miles (6 km) south of Nailsworth lands you at the spectacular Westonbirt Arboretum. It's more than trees: Hike the trails, stick around for an evening concert, check their calendar and take advantage of the special events. Continue to Malmesbury, built on several levels high above the River Avon. Your loop then takes a turn to the north. From Tetbury, another tidy town, head to Cirencester; the Corinuim Museum showcases Roman mosaics unearthed nearby.

Have a look at the 17th-century weavers' cottages in pretty Bilbury before spending some time at Chedworth Roman Villa—one of the largest in England. Wind up (and down!) at Cheltenham's Royal Oak Inn: lovely atmosphere and well-prepared food.

travelwise

Start Cheltenham   **End** Cheltenham   **Distance** 75 miles (121 km)
Roads A46, A433, B4425, minor roads
Insider Tip This wedge of England is well known for its wealth of pubs—on main streets and tucked off the beaten path. Stop a couple of times along the way for some fish and chips, shepherd's pie, a ploughman's lunch, and a pint of ale.

Shining through an abundance of foliage, Sudeley Castle is surrounded by nine gardens.

indre river ride

Extreme châteaus • Waterside villages • Local baskets

Driving west to east, it doesn't take long for you to be stopped in your tracks by the turreted and romantic Château d'Ussé. Another "oh wow" former residence along the way is Château Azay-le-Rideau, sitting on an island in the river. After that, the highlights become more humble but no less interesting.

In Villaines-les-Rochers, a village noted for its baskets made from rushes that grow beside the Indre. The 16th-century manor houses in Saché are set among chestnut trees. To flee from his creditors, Balzac moved here and, in 1835, penned *Le Père Goriot;* the writer's home is now a museum. From Saché to Montbazon, scenery highlights include orchards, mills, and villages. Farther east, the charming little town of Cormery is worth a stop for its 12th-century church and famed macaroon cookies.

A short detour delivers you to Montrésor with an 11th-century fortress that encloses a restored 16th-century fortress. Loches, a perched town with a medieval core, is a grand finale.

travelwise

Start Rigny-Ussé **End** Loches **Distance** 50 miles (80 km)
Roads D7, D17, D57, D217, D25, local roads
Insider Tip In Cormery—near the abbey—the Auberge du Mail has a delightful terrace shaded by lime trees and wisteria. It's the perfect spot to enjoy a well-prepared lunch capped off by some of the best macaroons around.

Château de Montrésor is richly furnished with antiques.

Cobblestone streets and Old World charm draw admirers to Rothenburg ob der Tauber.

romantic road trip

Historic towns • Engaging museums • Exquisite churches

Given the wealth of highlights and guaranteed traffic (this is Germany's top vacation route), leave at least three days for this north–south trip. Tauberbischofsheim, a medieval wine village, sets the historic/charming tone for the journey. Next up are the spa town of Bad Mergentheim, Weikersheim's moated castle, the altarpiece in Creglingen, Detwang's church, and peerless Rothenburg ob der Tauber.

The old marketplace and cloisters in medieval Feuchtwangen provide an open-air venue for summer performances. Farther on is Dinkelsbühl, preserved within walls and towers. En route to Nördlingen the landscape is nearly devoid of woodland— the result of a giant meteorite that passed this way some 15 million years ago.

From Nördlingen it isn't long before you reach the Danube, at Donauwörth. Just short of Füssen sits one of Germany's greatest romantic sights: King Ludwig II's castle Neuschwanstein.

travelwise

Start Würzburg **End** Füssen **Distance** 220 miles (354 km)
Roads Romantic Road (Romantische Strasse), B25, B17, local roads
Don't Miss Deutsches Haus, a grand old gabled merchant house in Dinkelsbühl, and a stroll around the city ramparts • Vistas from the church tower in Nördlingen • The bird's-eye view of the Neuschwanstein castle from the Marienbrücke footbridge

The lavish castle of Hluboká nad Vltavou in the Czech Republic stands elegant, reflecting neo-Gothic style.

CZECH REPUBLIC

the castle route

True Bohemia • Fortified strongholds • River valley and mountain views

Just north of Ceské Budejovice you come to the lofty castle of Hluboká nad Vltavou, one of the royal Schwarzenberg family's neo-Gothic fantasies. About 15 miles (24 km) north, bear left toward Písek. Head north on minor roads to Zvíkov, built in the 13th century—note the formidable round tower—on a wooded promontory.

Heading northwest along the Vltava River, you come to Orlík, rebuilt in the second half of the 19th century as a somewhat preposterous neo-Gothic fantasy. Return south the way you came, then head west to Blatná, known for its castle. From here, head south to Vimperk, a village that cowers under a crag.

Make your way 22 miles (35 km) east, toward Ceské Budejovice, for a stop in the town of Rozmberk nad Vltavou and a visit to its namesake castle. The final stop, Cervená Lhota, holds the most exquisite structure of all. Tucked in remote, wooded countryside is an islet reached by a cobblestone causeway. On the islet is a rust red 16th-century manor house that was built where a castle once stood.

travelwise

Start Ceské Budejovice   **End** Cervená Lhota   **Distance** 233 miles (375 km)
Roads Routes 105, 39, several minor roads
Don't Miss Zvikov, the king of Czech castles • The graffitoed facade of Rozmberk nad Vltavou castle • Conspicuously unpompous Cervená Lhota manor

historic routes

62
Following Lewis and Clark, North and South Dakota

A 400-mile (644 km) loop out of Bismarck, North Dakota, hugs the banks of the Mississippi and serves as an early American picture book, spotlighting indigenous history. One example: For thousands of years, Native Americans hunted and gathered in the region of Knife River Indian Villages National Historic Site. There are displays and re-creations that celebrate a very impressive culture. When to go: spring through fall.
www.lewisandclarktrail.com

63
Path of the Conquerors, Yucatán, Mexico

In the 16th century Spanish fleets in search of a route to the East instead found Aztec settlements and lots of gold. Today's traveler can make a 50-mile (80 km) drive from Quiahuiztlán to Boca del Río and see tiny fishing villages, ancient temples, the ruins of Spanish strongholds, and bustling Veracruz. Note: A few decades ago, Boca del Río was a simple fishing village; today, in addition to beaches, the city serves up fine restaurants and museums.
www.visitmexico.com

64
Via Appia Antica, Italy

Walk or bike along the rutted hand-hewn-basalt byway where chariots and carts covered ground (also slowly) many centuries ago. The ancient road takes you straight out of Rome; the starting point is not far from the Colosseum. The Catacombs of San Callisto help cement you to the past (take the 40-minute guided tour). Note: On a summer Saturday or Sunday, lunch among the locals at the Appia Antica Caffé; you can also rent a bicycle here.
www.parcoappiaantica.it

65
Driving the Mandarin Road, Vietnam

The 56-mile (90 km) stretch of Highway 1 between Hue and Danang is a history-soaked stretch. The route begins inland, heads through the mountains (great views of the South China Sea), and winds up at the Bay of Danang. Bonus: If you have time, head 17 miles (27 km) south of Danang to the ancient trading port town of Hoi An, which also offers very contemporary nightlife.
www.vietnamtourism.com

A traditional sod house at Fort Abraham Lincoln State Park, Mandan, ND

ROMANIA

66

transylvania spin

Village after village • Ancient dance • Medieval buildings

Visit Rasinari's village museum, then head to Orlat, a village dominated by a 14th-century earth fortress. Stop in Sibiu for a look at the Biserica Sf. Treime, a church that appears Catholic on its exterior though the interior has a Byzantine flavor. On the church grounds is an icon museum. The adjoining town of Saliste is one of the best places to see ancient Transylvanian dance performed exclusively by men.

In Tilisca, where most houses are wooden, stands a medieval citadel on a fortress that once belonged to a famous opponent of Julius Caesar. Continuing on through the Cindrel Mountains you'll reach Jina, one of the most remote and wealthiest of the route's villages. Continue on to see Dealul Cetatii, the remains of one of the region's finest ancient citadels. At the end of the itinerary is Cetatea Câlnic, a World Heritage site and area cultural center.

travelwise

Start Rasinari **End** Cetatea Câlnic
Distance 66 miles (106 km); 4WD vehicle recommended
Roads 106D, 106E, 67C, DN1, DN7, 106F
Insider Tip Try *varza a la Cluj,* the Romanian version of lasagna: baked layers of finely shredded cabbage and minced meat mixed with sour cream, rice, and bacon.

Traditional wooden windmills are on view at the ASTRA Ethnographic Museum in Sibiu, Romania.

Amid an arid landscape are the medieval ruins of the city of Mistrás in Peloponnesus.

peloponnesus

Odd tower houses • River caves • Castle ruins

A drive around this Peloponnese finger of land begins with a gas tank fill-up on Areópoli. Follow signs to Spilia Dirou—caves that are part of a subterranean river. Retrace your route then head south. On the western leg of the route you'll spot square tower houses and pass villages with beautiful Byzantine chapels.

   A circular detour delivers you to the tiny village of Mezapos. Take a stroll and admire the views across the sea to the 13th-century Tigani fortress. When you reach the village of Alika, look for a right turn marked Váthia, a worthwhile stop for its stone tower houses.

   Continue on along the east coast, through several villages and past quiet beaches. On the final stretch to the port town of Gíthio, the road passes to the south of the Taygetos Mountains. A side trip north lands you in Mistrás, a ruined Byzantine city; the castle affords great views.

travelwise

Start Areópoli **End** Githio **Distance** 70 miles (113 km)
Roads Local roads, Highway 39
Insider Tip Food—from grilled meat to phyllo pastry tarts—is a delightful component of this trip. At the end point, Gíthio, chow down on the catch of the day or small-plate snacks (*mezedes*) at Ouzerie Korali, on the town's main square.

On the lookout, two cheetah brothers stand atop a large termite mound.

68

wild okavango

Animals great and small • Parks • Dreamy lodges

Hit the road sometime between May and October. Stock up on water, snacks, and gas before you head out in your 4x4!

The starting point, Maun, is Botswana's fifth largest town, a favorite stomping ground for donkeys and goats that aren't shy about hanging around the curbside produce sellers. Leaving Maun, look for signs to Sherobe, 29 miles (47 km) away. Take the turnoff for Okavango River Lodge and Crocodile Camp if you want to take a boat trip through delta wetlands.

Moermi Game Reserve—a national park—may well be Africa's most captivating wildlife sanctuary. You could easily spend several days here—camping or staying at a lodge—while you indulge in wildlife spottings, from lions to giraffes.

You'll enter sprawling Chobe National Park—with one of the largest concentrations of game in Africa—at its south entrance, Mababe Gate. The end point of the trip is Savuti, a campground and lodge area within the park. Wildlife reigns here. Get ready to come upon the likes of elephants and wildebeest.

travelwise

Start Maun **End** Savuti
Distance 137 miles (220 km)
Roads Local roads
Insider Tip Only as long as the rivers stay wild (no dams) and no fences block animal migration, can the delta remain one of Earth's greatest wild places.

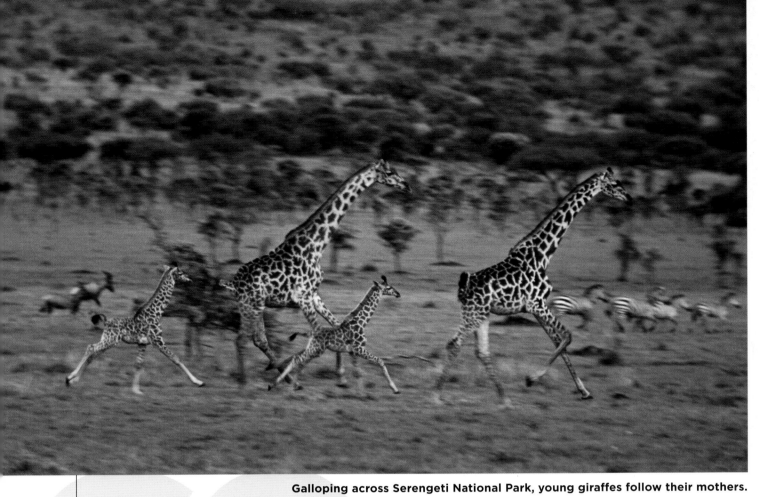

Galloping across Serengeti National Park, young giraffes follow their mothers.

69

serengeti safari

The Maasai people • A beyond-belief crater • Migrations of millions

This is a 4WD adventure with a powerful lure early on. At Lake Manyara National Park seek out the pink flamingos and blue monkeys (OK, gray elephants, too). At Oldeani the highway slowly climbs the fertile southern slope of Ngorongoro Crater; at Heroes Point you'll get your first peek at the enormous crater's interior.

From this high point the road heads steeply down to the Serengeti region, a land of brown semidesert. Before long you reach famous Olduvai Gorge, where, in 1931, Mary and Louis Leakey discovered human remains dating back some two million years.

An hour's drive west gets you to Serengeti National Park, a place where zebra and wildebeest roam. Situated in the heart of the park is Seronera. This end-of-the-journey settlement offers lodges, campgrounds, and some of the area's best game viewing.

travelwise

Start Arusha   **End** Seronera   **Distance** 187 miles (301 km)
Roads Tanzania A104, B144
Insider Tip Schedule your visit for January, February, or sometime between June and October; check online for wildebeest migration maps. No matter when you plan to go, book overnight accommodations way in advance.

driving the dmz

Combat landmarks • Regenerated eucalyptus groves • Farm villages

Given the unexploded bombs and land mines still in the area some 40 years after the Vietnam War ended, an expert guide is a must for this trip along the demilitarized zone. The Ben Hai River starting point is the former line of demarcation between North and South Vietnam along the 17th parallel. A no-man's-land during the war, the DMZ stretched north and south of the riverbank for 3 miles (5 km) in either direction. Memorials line the river; the rebuilt Hien Luong Bridge, destroyed by U.S. bombers in 1967, is perhaps the most moving among them.

On the main road west of Cam Lo, a trail leads up to the summit of Firebase Fuller, from which U.S. artillery hurled shells as far as Khe Sanh, 25 miles (40 km) southwest. Climbing past farm villages, the route sees a lot of truck traffic out of Laos. A marker on the Dakrong Bridge memorializes a spur of the Ho Chi Minh Trail, which intersected Route 9 here. Eight miles (13 km) west, the road twists into Khe Sanh, the DMZ's largest U.S. combat base.

travelwise

Start Ben Hai River   **End** Khe Sanh   **Distance** 63 miles (101 km)
Roads Highway 1, Route 9
Insider Tip Tour guides not only keep travelers safe from unexploded land mines and bombs, they can share riveting stories about what transpired here in the 1960s.

Traveling on the back of a water buffalo, a boy rides past rice paddy fields.

cordillera terraces

Ancient rice terraces • Challenging treks • Native wines

The star on this journey: some of the most remarkable man-made landscapes on the planet. The rice terraces that striate the Cordillera Mountain area, which dominates the north-central portion of Luzon Island, were carved nearly 2,000 years ago, making them ancient works of art.

Beyond Baguio, make your way to Halsema Highway, which soon heads up the mountains, affording vistas of bright green farm terraces cloaking steep mountainsides. The ascent continues past Sayangan to the aptly named Highest Point (7,200 feet, 2,195 m) before winding downhill. Seasoned trekkers can tackle Mount Ampacao; the trail begins at the Ambasing Elementary School in Sagada.

The road and the Chico River pretty much run parallel en route to Bontoc, the Cordillera region's historic capital. Cross the Chico Bridge and stop in Samoki, a town known for its woven goods. Next up are the trip's most spectacular sights: the Banaue river terraces, which stretch as far as the eye can see.

travelwise

Start Baguio City   **End** Banaue   **Distance** 80 miles (129 km)
Roads Magsaysay Avenue, La Trinidad Avenue, Halsema Highway, local roads
Don't Miss Ifugao Province's green, green Banaue rice terraces, cut centuries ago and irrigated by streams and springs • The native rice wine and sugarcane wine • Ifugao dance and music at the Banaue Hotel

**Opposite: A small village hides among rice terraces and looming mountain ranges.
Below: Colorful bromeliads stand out against dense fog on the mountainside of Banaue.**

TAIWAN

72

taroko gorge

Marble cliffs • Enchanting waterfalls • Interestingly named sights

Once inside the park, look for the signposted trail leading to Eternal Spring Shrine, an enchanting tableau that includes a sonorous waterfall and a classic Chinese-design structure backdropped by mountains. Swallow Grotto is a section of the road where a long tunnel was blasted through the cliff. To lure back the namesake birds that nested in the grottoes but were driven out by traffic, the authorities made this a pedestrians-only section of the road.

Beyond Indian Rock is the twisting Tunnel of Nine Turns, a series of short tunnels cut through sheer marble. Taroko's drama reaches its peak here: The gorge squeezes between cliffs; tiered waterfalls rumble along the Liwu River.

Just over a mile (2 km) beyond the Bridge of Motherly Devotion and before you reach the resort town of Tianxiang, a suspension bridge leads to the six-story Heavenly Summit Pagoda. Climb to the top for some outstanding views.

travelwise

Start Taroko National Park Headquarters   **End** Tianxiang
Distance 14 miles (23 km)
Road Highway 8/Central Cross Island Highway
Insider Tip Taroko National Park Headquarters has snacks, maps, and weather-condition notices posted by the park rangers. It's also a good place to learn about park flora, including some 300 species of butterflies.

A forest clearing frames the base of a pagoda in Taroko Gorge.

An aerial view shows the white-sand beaches, hiking trails, and beautiful landscapes of Sai Kung Country Park in Hong Kong.

driving sai kung

Coastal views • Seaside restaurants • Hiking and camping

This scenic, winding northeast route not far from Hong Kong follows the coast into Sai Kung Country Park. Past villa- and boat-filled Marina Cove, the road opens to views of the wide bay at Pak Sha Wan. The highway then snakes past villages, wooded areas, and garden nurseries en route to the town Sai Kung, the area's main community.

The Country Park Visitor Center is home to a small museum that showcases coral found off the coast. Next on the traveler's radar screen is Wong Shek Pier, offering sublime mountain views. From here, a ferry ride away, the island of Tap Mun Chau bustles with fishermen. Have a look at the Tin Hau Temple, notable for its porcelain roof figurines. Another highlight, Balanced Rock—a weird rock formation—sits just off the island's southeastern tip. Be sure you've checked the ferry schedule for your return to Wong Shek Pier.

travelwise

Start Hiram Highway at Clear Water Bay Road   **End** Wong Shek Pier
Distance 11 miles (18 km)
Roads Hiram's Highway, Po Tung, Tai Mong Tsai, Sai Sha roads
Insider Tip Be sure to visit the Sia Kung Country Park Visitor Center to learn about the park's flora and fauna and the area's traditional ways of life.

driving the catlins

Fossilized forest • Yellow-eyed penguins • Crashing waves

The road—coastal and winding—runs through the region known as the Catlins, characterized by forests, beaches, waterfalls, and wildlife.

Pull over at Waipapa Point and take in the golden beach and lighthouse. Continue east to Slope Point, the southernmost point on New Zealand's South Island. Head on to Curio Bay, where low tide exposes a 180-million-year-old fossilized forest with rocks bearing the imprints of ferns. Yellow-eyed penguins nest here, while at adjoining Porpoise Bay dolphins can be spotted in summer.

Right off the main road, Matai Falls are the easiest cascades to reach on this trip. A 10-minute walk lands you at Horseshoe Falls, from which the Matai Falls are also visible. Purakaunui Falls, the most dramatic, are reached via a lengthy gravel-path drive followed by a short walk.

Just beyond Owaka township, turn off to Cannibal Bay, where Hooker's sea lions often can be seen. Keep your distance; they can charge with surprising speed. More yellow-eyed penguins can be seen at Roaring Bay and Nugget Point, which also has a dramatically perched lighthouse. Kaka Point, a summer resort favorite, is the last town of note before Balclutha.

travelwise

Start Invercargill **End** Balclutha **Distance** 99 miles (159 km)
Road Highway 92
Insider Tip Located at a particularly pretty portion, the Nugget Point Hotel and Spa offers a fine extend-your-stay option. Spend the night or simply submit to a massage.

Opposite: A lighthouse waits for the rising sun off the cliff on Nugget Point, New Zealand.
Below: Traveling to the southern point of New Zealand is as far south as you can go—or is it?

moun
meanders

tain

Reflections of mountains and a road bridge stretch over Lake Sylvenstein in Germany.

In the former gold rush town of Skagway, Alaska, the streets are lined with colorful wooden shops.

CANADA AND ALASKA

yukon circle

Wide-open landscapes • Grizzly bears • Historic haunts

Begin in Whitehorse, capital of the Yukon Territory and important gold rush landmark. Take a paddle-wheeler spin on the Yukon River, visit the Yukon Transportation Museum, check out what locals say is the world's largest weather vane.

Go west out of town along the Yukon Plateau. The visuals become dramatic along the ramparts of the Kluane Ranges, which dwarf the crossroads town of Haines Junction and extend along the eastern front of Kluane National Park and Reserve.

Driving northwest along enormous Kluane Lake you'll reach the ghost town of Silver City, built during the short-lived 1904 gold rush.

Tutchone natives fish for several sorts of salmon near Klukshu, one of the Yukon's oldest settlements. After the highway climbs into British Columbia, the Chilkat Pass is where the dramatic plunge to Haines, Alaska, begins. From Haines take the ferry to Skagway for some culture amid the wilds.

travelwise

Start Whitehorse   **End** Whitehorse   **Distance** 525 miles (845 km)
Roads Canada Highways 1, 3, Alaska Highways 7, 98, Canada Highways 2, 1; this route includes a ferry
Insider Tip At Skagway's Haven Café, a local favorite, fuel up on soups, sandwiches, good coffee, fresh baked goods, and made-on-the-spot milkshakes.

blue ridge parkway

Waterfall hikes • Views, views, views • Folk art

The age-old beauty of the southern Appalachians plays out all along this popular byway. After a brief climb the road gracefully rises and falls along the forested spine of the Blue Ridge. Midway to Roanoke, at the historic James River, the road sees its lowest elevation (649 feet, 198 m). South of Roanoke, farmland rules the views. The fire tower atop Groundhog Mountain yields excellent views of the high country. Grandfather Mountain (5,964 feet, 1,818 m), the highest in the Blue Ridge, is one of the oldest in the world. Get onto U.S. 221, which twists up to a visitor center and spectacular views. The S-shaped Linn Cove Viaduct was built to help preserve Grandfather's fragile environment.

Enjoy the parade of views, but take time out at the Folk Art Center in Asheville. You can also detour to the magnificent Biltmore Estate. A series of stunning mountain peaks signals the trip's finale.

travelwise

Start Rockfish Gap, Virginia **End** Great Smoky Mountains National Park, North Carolina **Distance** 469 miles (755 km)
Road Blue Ridge Parkway
Don't Miss Moses H. Cone Memorial Park • A waterfall hike at Linville Falls, near the viaduct • The traditional mountain crafts and music at the Folk Art Center

Autumn leaves encompass a quiet stretch of the Blue Ridge Parkway.

MONTANA AND WYOMING

beartooth highway

Rocky Mountain moments • Scenic switchbacks • Alpine tundra

At the start of the trip, Beartooth Plateau—a hulking block of metamorphic rock—looms over the prairie foothills. Soon it is all about cliff vistas and dramatic switchbacks.

As you approach the turnoff for Island Lake Campground, two towering spires come into view: Pilot Peak and Index Peak. A short ways on, Beartooth Lake, nestled against cliffs, is a great picnic spot.

When the road breaks out of the trees, look left across the canyon to see Beartooth Falls. Two or three minutes after that, follow the gravel road to Clay Butte Lookout, a fire tower that commands a smashing view of some of Montana's highest mountains. As the road heads down the flank of the plateau, keep an eye out for deer, elk, and moose. An unmarked bridge over Lake Creek takes you to a short path that leads to a powerful waterfall. As the trip winds down, the northeast entrance to Yellowstone National Park awaits.

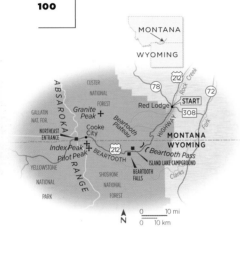

travelwise

Start Red Lodge **End** Yellowstone National Park **Distance** 69 miles (111 km)
Road U.S. 212
Insider Tip Red Lodge, Montana, is a town that loves to party. Oktoberfest and Halloween are favorite excuses for unbridled fun, though that's just the beginning.

A stream in Hellroaring Plateau, Montana, reflects clouds and the setting sun.

In Trinidad, the Crocodile House was previously an industrialist's home but now is a popular tourist destination.

cuba's southwest

Pristine mountain scenery • Inviting Caribbean Sea • Lesser known Cuba

Exit the unspoiled colonial town of Trinidad and drive west. Three miles (5 km) on, follow the road north toward Topes de Collantes and begin the ascent into the Sierra del Escambray. The Topes de Collantes nature reserve teems with grottoes, canyons, natural pools, hummingbirds, woodpeckers, orchids, ferns, and the national flower: the butterfly lily. Continue north and east for about 8 miles (13 km) of breathtaking scenery visible through gaps in the forest. The road then corkscrews down. The orange groves around Cumanayagua sometimes offer up heady fragrance. Beyond, citrus fades to golden grassland grazed by humped cattle.

Reaching the coast, you'll see Hacienda La Vega, a cattle farm. Toward the end of the loop trip you'll pass rivers, ravines, and sparkling white-sand beaches. Nine miles (14 km) beyond the Río Cabagán the road offers a final rise back to Trinidad.

travelwise

Start Trinidad **Finish** Trinidad **Distance** 96 miles (154 km)
Roads Circuito Sur coastal road, Route 4-206, local roads
Don't Miss A hike through a coffee plantation and past farmhouses to Caburni Falls in Topes de Collantes • The 5-mile (8 km) side trip to Embalse Hanabanilla for lunch at Hotel Hanabanilla, built on the edge of a grand lake • A visit to the Crocodile House, an elegant 18th-century Trinidad residence

PUERTO RICO

79

the panoramic route

Coffee plantations • Gorges • Swimming holes

One of the Caribbean's premier scenic drives, the Panoramic Route is best done over two days. Head west—inland—from Maunabo before starting the climb into the foothills. Small settlements dot the way, as do bamboo, tree ferns, banana plants, and cattle. After about 6 miles (10 km) from home base the road climbs past coffee plantations.

You drive through Reserva Forestal Carite, 6,000 acres (2,430 ha) of rain forest, home to waterfalls, 50 species of birds, and the blue pool known as Charco Azul. After you leave the jungle, the views open up on both sides of the road. Pretty soon you reach a high point at Mirador Piedra Degetau. Next on the agenda is Aibonito, the highest town in Puerto Rico. Beyond is the Cañon San Cristóbal, the island's deepest gorge.

Twisting and turning scenically along the spine of the Cordillera Central, the route goes through another large forest (Toro Negro) before coming to a prime in-the-woods swimming hole at the Area de Recreo Doña Juana.

travelwise

Start Maunabo **End** Mayagüez
Distance 120 miles (193 km)
Roads The route is marked at most junctions—but not all—with "RUTA," as in La Ruta Panorámica
Insider Tip Take a guided hike through Cañon San Cristóbal.

Mangroves jut out of a restoration project in Cabo Rojo.

Along the coast a secluded house finds refuge among sand and palm trees.

DOMINICAN REPUBLIC

cordillera samaná

Mighty waterfall • Palm-fringed beaches • Grand mountain scenery

Just west of town you'll see the junction for El Limón. Head that way, snaking uphill and back and you take in the first fine views of the trip. Los Haitises National Park will appear to be afloat on the hazy horizon, and the coast tantalizes.

Be on guard for potholes as you head down toward El Limón, where you head north on a dirt road to Playa Morón, an orange-sand beach. Head back to El Limón on your way to Playa Punta Popy, a magnet for kiteboarders. Playa las Ballenas is the next stunning beach on the route. Park your vehicle, don a snorkel, and hit the surf. Stop for grilled seafood at Playa Bonita.

The final stretch of the trip is a southwest drive that takes you around switchbacks . . . and over potholes. At Viverto Las Colinas a plant nursery clings to the mountainside. The landscape beyond the village of Los Puentes includes isolated, rounded hills called *mogotes*. It is downhill—steeply in sections—from here to Sánchez.

travelwise

Start Samaná **End** Sánchez **Distance** 31 miles (50 km)
Roads Follow local roads and road signs
Insider Tip A visit to the magnificent Salto del Limón waterfall requires advanced planning, an excursion reservation with the El Limón concern Santi Rancho, and a willingness to brave rough terrain.

north of penonomé

White churches · Citrus plantations · Wide valley vistas

The road is punctuated with ruts and washed-out spots, so 4WD is the best way to experience this otherwise breezy trip. Just past agricultural La Pintada, the Charco las Lavanderas natural pools are touted for their healing powers.

After this stretch, the going gets tougher as you head into ever more rugged terrain. Admire the view west toward the sheer-walled mesa known as Cerro Orari.

Farther on, the volcanic Cerro Chichibalí (sometimes wreathed in clouds) stands imposingly to the northeast. You'll descend through cattle pastures and conifer forests to Churuquita Grande. Spectacular limestone formations challenge you to stay focused on the road as you continue past a charming little church on your way to Posada Cerro La Vieja, where eco-adventures and well-earned spa treatments await.

travelwise

Start Penonomé **End** Posada Cerro La Vieja **Distance** 32 miles (51 km)
Roads There are no primary named or numbered roads; follow intersection signs
Insider Tip There are impostor "Panama" hats and then there's the real thing. Score an authentic handmade *sombrero pintado* from a vendor at the colonial plaza in Penonomé

A blue-crowned motmot rests on a branch in Central America (left). Panama's Queen of Carnival greets the crowd (right).

COLOMBIA

coffee country

Deep-valley vistas • Hats and more hats • Colonial towns

Much of this route is officially designated a "Ruta Escénica" (scenic route). You soon see why. Beyond the town of Caldas, you snake up through pine forests to emerge on a ridgetop studded with villages. Vast views take in pretty valleys. From the often-in-the-clouds village of Santa Barbara, the road snakes down into a broad valley of emerald pastures.

Follow the sign for Aguadas. Veer uphill past the hamlet of La Lorena and the quaint colonial village of Armas.

From here the road clings to a precipitous mountainside rife with coffee bushes as it approaches the delightful hillside town of Aguadas, whose denizens craft broad-rim hats from palm fronds. The next worth-a-stroll is Pácora. You reach the town of Salamina—a National Monument—after what feels like a roller-coaster ride past tropical foliage and sugarcane fields. En route to Manizales you'll drive through a narrow valley shaded by bamboo.

travelwise

Start Medellín   **End** Manizales   **Distance** 145 miles (233 km)
Roads Highway 25, local roads
Don't Miss Fueling up in Medellín with locally sourced coffee at LeBon, a café that also serves breakfast • In Aguadas, the hundreds of traditional hats at the Museo Nacional de Sombrero • Salamina's colonial church

Traditional houses in the coffee-producing area, or Zona Cafetera, of Colombia

The distant peaks of the Andes provide a snowy backdrop in Patagonia.

pure patagonia

Unspoiled lakes • Pretty sheep farms • Amazing mountain vistas

At the start of this route is San Carlos de Bariloche, a quaint town at the foot of the Andes with quite the nightlife, good shopping, and excellent fare.

Heading south you pass a string of lakes in Parque Nacional Nahuel Huapi and the town of El Bolsón, boasting a fine street market. Next, the road climbs past fruit farms: raspberries, strawberries, apples, pears, and more. Next up: Estancia Leleque, a unique historical museum.

Farther on, Trevelin, a Welsh settlement, was damaged by volcanic eruptions in 2008; occasional eruptions continue. If you want to stretch your legs on a scenic hike, Parque Nacional Los Alerces is the place to do it. A dusty gravel road leads north to RN 40 and the end of the route. Along the way, stop just outside Cholila, where a modest cabin was the home of Butch Cassidy and the Sundance Kid in the early 1900s.

travelwise

Start San Carlos de Bariloche   **End** San Carlos de Bariloche
Distance 384 miles (618 km)
Roads RN 40, RN 259, RP 71
Insider Tip You can fish for trophy trout, hike, ride a horse, or just enjoy the scenery and food at Campo Cielo, on a lake with comfy tent accommodations.

MORE TO SEE

winding wine roads

84

Strongholds of the Middle Ages, Portugal

An 87-mile (140 km) loop out of Guarda links a quartet of fortified medieval villages. The landscape morphs from orchards and vineyards to boulder-strewn slopes, dotted palace ruins, and, toward the end of the trip, granite boars (two of these rock mammals guard the fortress-village of Castelo Mendo). Tasty tidbit: Feijoada, the rich stew associated with Brazil, has roots here in Portugal's northeast.
www.visitcentro.com

85

Langhe Valley, Piedmont, Italy

Wine is central to the lure of the Langhe, but so are the sweet villages that punctuate the fertile landscapes. Start in Alba and weave your way along country roads back to Alba, being sure to take in Diano d'Alba (a 16th-century parish church), Barolo (truly fine wines), and the striking village of Serralunga d'Alba. Guilty pleasure: Take the waters at Acqui Terme.
www.italia.it

86

Classic Wine Road, Plesivica, Croatia

Wind through the countryside between Jastrebarsko and Samobor. The first half of the 19-mile (31 km) trip is particularly wine-centric; the tail end of the route spotlights the picturesque Samobor Hills. Tasty tip: Stop off for cream pudding or (and!) a slice of *potica*—a walnut-filled sweet yeast bread.
www.croatia.hr

87

Wheat Fields and Vineyards, Swartland, South Africa

The fertile "black country" is named for an indigenous shrub that turns black in winter. Head out of Darling for the 90-mile (145 km) trip along Shiraz-producing vineyards. In the village of Riebeek Kasteel, galleries, restaurants, and cafés line the town square. Timing: On the first Saturday of the month, the Riebeek Valley morning market brims with fresh regional produce.
www.swartlandwineroute
.co.za

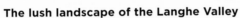

The lush landscape of the Langhe Valley

Sheep graze in the green, rural countryside of Northern Ireland.

sperrin mountains

Wild beauty • Ideal trails • Dreamy villages

Mountain hares and hikers dot the lush, green Sperrin Mountains. You will have no choice but to park your vehicle and follow in their footsteps. Some 6 miles (10 km) into the trip, a marked scenic drive leads you to the beautiful conifers of Gortin Glen Forest Park. As you slip into Gortin, splendid views mark the way. On the northern side of the Owenkillew River are some of the best: Barnes Gap opens onto fabulous vistas across the Glenelly Valley to the highest Sperrin peaks.

The charming Sperrin Heritage Centre tells the story of the area's wildlife, geological history, and rich cultural lore. Turn left at Sperrin village to cross the moorland heart of the hills. At Cranagh, turn right along the B47 for the lovely 7-mile (11 km) run to pretty Plumbridge; the B48 brings you back to where you began: Omagh.

travelwise

Start Omagh **End** Omagh **Distance** 70 miles (113 km)
Roads B48, B46, B47, B44, local roads
Insider Tip In the village of Gortin, stop at the well-run Badoney Tavern—a walkers' hangout whose owners can supply great local intelligence as well as a fortifying meal

Rievaulx Abbey's ancient Gothic arches stand tall on the side of a peaceful valley in North York Moors National Park.

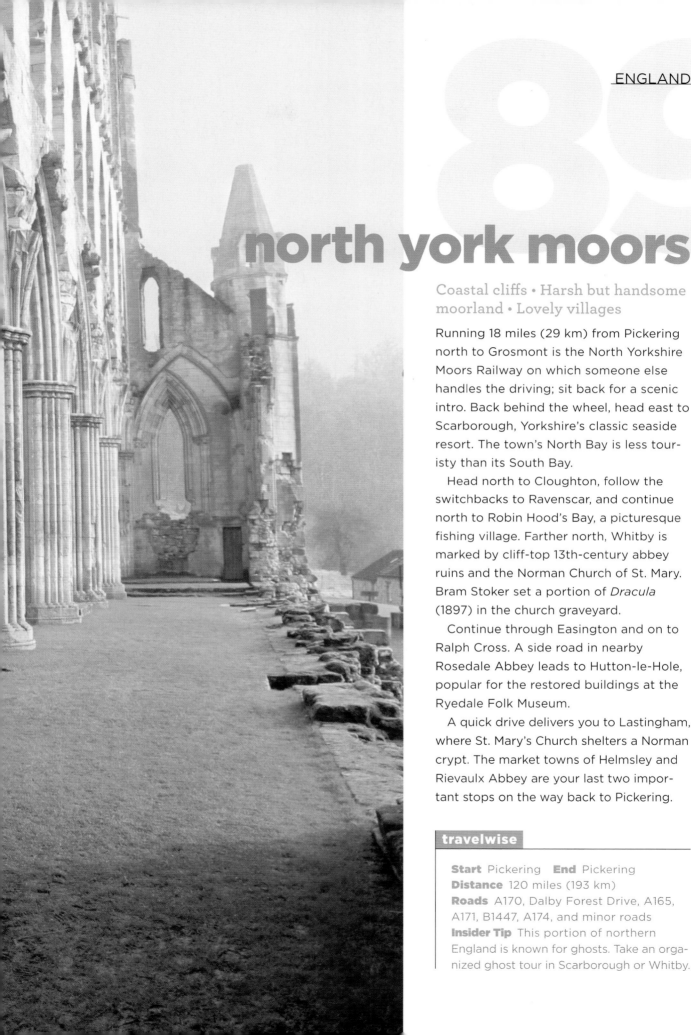

north york moors

Coastal cliffs • Harsh but handsome moorland • Lovely villages

Running 18 miles (29 km) from Pickering north to Grosmont is the North Yorkshire Moors Railway on which someone else handles the driving; sit back for a scenic intro. Back behind the wheel, head east to Scarborough, Yorkshire's classic seaside resort. The town's North Bay is less touristy than its South Bay.

Head north to Cloughton, follow the switchbacks to Ravenscar, and continue north to Robin Hood's Bay, a picturesque fishing village. Farther north, Whitby is marked by cliff-top 13th-century abbey ruins and the Norman Church of St. Mary. Bram Stoker set a portion of *Dracula* (1897) in the church graveyard.

Continue through Easington and on to Ralph Cross. A side road in nearby Rosedale Abbey leads to Hutton-le-Hole, popular for the restored buildings at the Ryedale Folk Museum.

A quick drive delivers you to Lastingham, where St. Mary's Church shelters a Norman crypt. The market towns of Helmsley and Rievaulx Abbey are your last two important stops on the way back to Pickering.

travelwise

Start Pickering **End** Pickering
Distance 120 miles (193 km)
Roads A170, Dalby Forest Drive, A165, A171, B1447, A174, and minor roads
Insider Tip This portion of northern England is known for ghosts. Take an organized ghost tour in Scarborough or Whitby.

Submerged by a dam in Parque Nacional da Peneda-Gerês, the village of Vilarinho das Furnas surfaces only when the reservoir falls.

PORTUGAL

90

country roads

Rugged mountains • Verdant riverbanks • Family-run vineyards

Fine scenery is the theme of this pleasant rural drive. After you head out of Ponte de Lima you will see grapevine-draped pergolas and rows of white-grape vines.

En route to Parque Nacional da Peneda-Gerês, you'll pass the pretty village of Arcos de Valdevez, pine and eucalyptus groves, rockier terrain of heather, and terraced hillsides. A small visitor center and ancient megaliths sit not far from the park's entrance. Head down to Soajo, site of 24 raised stone granaries.

Head toward Gavieira, past black sheep, horses, goats, and longhorn cattle. About a 5-minute drive past the village of Adrao is one of the drive's best lookout points, with views of sheer granite slopes, verdant valleys, and a sprinkling of hamlets.

After passing the roadside chapel at Paradela, you'll reach the Lima River and, soon, several dozen stone granaries grouped just outside Lindoso. Spend some time in the old town of Ponte da Barca, the drive's terminus.

travelwise

Start Ponte de Lima **End** Ponte da Barca **Distance** 63 miles (101 km)
Roads N202, N304, N203, local roads
Don't Miss The area's raised stone granaries—odd structures built to keep grain safe from small critters • Castelo de Lindoso (*lindoso* means "beautiful") • Riverside Ponte da Barca's open market hall and 15th-century bridge

along high hills

Terraced groves of citrus and olives • Fine landscapes • Strolls

Following the bay, head northwest out of Altea, past plantings of orange and lemon trees. The grand Serra de Guadalest (*serra* is Catalan for "sierra") looms in the distance. Beyond Callosa d'En Sarrià, a medieval architectural town, detour to Fonts d'Algar, an area of rushing springs.

From Callosa the road climbs limestone hills to the extraordinary Guadalest, perched on granite pinnacles. Wander the village and go through the tunnel that leads to the old part of town. Reach the castle ruins by following the "Museo" signs.

Next up is the pretty village of Confrides, which sits at the source of the Guadalest River. Have a look at the monumental walnut tree gracing the main square. The route's westernmost point is Penàguila, worth a stop for its medieval gateway and noble mansions. A drive through dense forest leads to Serra, with Roman ruins. Farther on is Finestrat, with views of the Mediterranean. The final stop, Albir, boasts a pretty beach and good hiking trails.

travelwise

Start Altea **End** Albir **Distance** 37 miles (59 km)
Roads N332, A150, CV755, CV70, CV770, CV781, CV785, CV758
Insider Tip Lost amid all the architectural and panoramic intensity in Guadalest is the Miniatures Museum with such delights as a Goya painting done on a grain of rice and a camel passing through the eye of a needle.

Water cascades from Fonts d'Algar (left). An old bell tower in Guadalest overlooks the mountainside (right).

a "grand canyon"

Exquisite pottery • Dramatic scenery • Lots of lavender

This loop begins (and ends) in a town famous for its faience pottery and medieval streets. Moustiers-Ste.-Marie has enough charm to keep you from the driver's seat. But resist. The Verdon Gorge is the cornerstone of a fabulous road trip.

Just beyond town, the road rises dramatically, then makes its way down a cliff, with the Verdon River far below. At Bélvèdere de Mayreste, your first view of the canyon waits in the wings. Access it by making your way up the rocks. Outside La Palud-sur-Verdon—a nexus of hiking, rafting, and climbing—pick up the D23 for a ride along the edge of a plateau before heading back to La Palud and then driving east.

Beyond Soleils, the route heads south and then west. Take time to see the castle in Trigance and the Pont de l'Artuby (loved by bungee jumpers). Beyond the Source de Vaumale, the road reaches its highest point before twisting down past Aiguines and Lac de Ste.-Croix, a short drive from Moustiers.

travelwise

Start Moustiers-Ste.-Marie **End** Moustiers-Ste.-Marie **Distance** 50 miles (80 km)
Roads D952, D23 (Route des Crêtes), D955, D90, D71, D957
Insider Tip Spend the night at 10-room Château-de-Trigance, or at least stop for lunch. The fare at this perched castle-turned-inn is deliciously local—with bread baked in the village just beyond the castle walls.

The sun casts its light into the Grand Canyon du Verdon.

In Germany's Upper Bavaria region, the iconic Ramsau church is blanketed in snow.

the alpine road

Entertaining landscapes • Alpine foothills • Classic Germany

Drive past Bernau to the vacation resort of Grassau, which sits in the shadow of the Hochplatte (5,204 feet, 1,586 m). Next up is Marquartstein, notable for its 11th-century castle and a ski lift up the Hochplatte. The road winds on to Reit im Winkl, a resort backed by forest-filled mountains rising to 6,500 feet (2,000 m).

The busy little town of Ruhpolding's fine baroque parish church protects a great treasure, the Ruhpolding Madonna, an early-13th-century wood carving. Directly east is Inzell, with an onion-dome church.

Just off the main road, the village of Ramsau retains its age-old charm. The parish church of 1512 stands on a rise against a background of snowcapped Alps. Park your vehicle and follow the sign that will lead you across the stream and to the perfect Ramsau photo op. It is tempting to continue west to Hintersee, a lake backdropped by peaks and a glacier. Double back to the main road and drive to the gorgeous town of Berchtesgaden.

travelwise

Start Autobahn exit 106: Prien-Bernau   **End** Berchtesgaden
Distance 63 miles (101 km)
Road Route 305
Insider Tip Stop at the Niedermayer bakery in Ramsau for pastries and coffee.

looping lovely lakes

Photo-op landscapes • Quaint farming villages • Classic covered bridge

Stop in the town of Vitznau and take the cog railroad up to Mount Rigi. Back behind the wheel, head to the lakeside resort of Weggis and its fine waterside promenade.

At the hairpin bend on Route 2, near Küssnacht, is the tiny stone Astrid Chapel. Set in a sweet garden, it was built as a memorial to Queen Astrid of Belgium, who was killed in 1935 when the car driven by King Leopold crashed into a pear tree.

Next stop is Luzern and the Swiss Museum of Transportation, the most popular museum in Switzerland. Stop for some locally made Ramseier, a nonalcoholic drink made from more than 30 apple varieties.

Look for signs pointing toward Beromünster, atop a steep hill. On the village's main street is the collegiate Church of St. Michael, which was built as a monastery in 981. Its tower, with a 13th-century pedigree, was rebuilt in the baroque style. Stop at the crow-step-gabled 16th-century Hotel Hirschen, to dine or spend the night. Off Hauptgasse is the so-called Schloss (castle), which was once a residential tower. It is thought that Switzerland's first printed matter was produced here in 1470 by Ulrich Gering, who went on to found the first printing press in France.

At Ballwil, turn left toward Sins. Keep an eye out for a classic covered bridge crossing the River Reuss. At Goldau, rejoin Route 2 for the last leg to Schwyz.

travelwise

Start Schwyz **End** Schwyz **Distance** 93 miles (150 km)
Roads Drive this loop clockwise. Route 2/8, Route 2B Route 2, Route 25
Insider Tip Choose a souvenir from the source. Schwyz is where Swiss Army knives are made. More than 25,000 of the classic tools are produced daily.

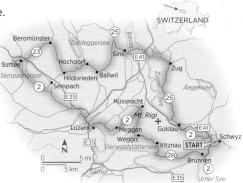

Opposite: The clear, tranquil waters of Lake Lucerne   Below: Zug's outdoor cafés

The beautiful rock formation Pravcická Brana

CZECH REPUBLIC

northern bohemia

Green valleys • Tidy villages • Spectacular rock formations

The village of Hrensko sits in a gorge edged by overhanging rocks. Beyond, deep in the woods is the Pravcická Brana, the largest natural stone bridge in central Europe. To visit, take the foot path from Mezni Louka. The hamlet of Mezná, perched above a gorge, can be forged via a wooden bridge. Rustic inns offer creature comforts— more of which await in Jetrichovice, a charming village with cozy guesthouses.

Continuing southward, the drab town of Ceska Kamenice is redeemed by its baroque chapel. Three miles (5 km) east is another fine rock formation. Panská Skála, which resembles a pipe organ, is made up of thousands of basalt columns. Two 16th-century castles are the highlights of Benesov and Ploucnici.

On the final stretch, highlights include the sandstone boulders at Tisá and the tabletop mountain called Decinsky Sneznik, accessible via hiking trails. Retrace your path and end at the enchanting Rose Garden in Decin.

travelwise

Start Hrensko   **End** Decin   **Distance** 70 miles (113 km)
Roads Local roads and Route 13
Insider Tip This part of the world is paradise for hikers, some of whom come upon fossils of sea animals along the trails. Millions of years ago there was a shallow sea here.

rural maramures

Handmade crafts • Traditional villages • Meadows and mountains

The journey begins with an uphill stint to Sisesti and a look at the Muzeul Memorial Vasile Lucaciu, a tribute to the Greco-Catholic priest who fought for the rights of ethnic Romanians in Transylvania.

In the village of Surdesti, the peal of church bells from Sf. Arhangheli signal the beginning and end of each haymaking day—a centuries-old tradition. Follow the signs for Biserica. At the end of a drive lined with walnut trees is the Sf. Arhangheli. Ask for the key at the parish house at the gate. Until recently, this was Europe's tallest wooden church.

Retrace your route, then head toward the winter resort of Cavnic. Look for a cliff on the left side of the road. You'll know it when you see it: It sports a painted Romanian flag. Hidden from the road is a cluster of boulders that resemble haystacks. Beyond the Neteda Pass, pull over for views of haystack-dotted meadows and the Carpathian peaks. Drive down the winding road past myrtle groves until you reach Budesti.

travelwise

Start Baia-Sprie   **End** Budesti   **Distance** 30 miles (48 km)
Roads DJ184 and local roads
Insider Tip A mile (under 2 km) before Budesti—one of the largest villages in the area—the road plays an optical-illusion trick on drivers. It seems to be heading uphill when, in fact, it is descending

Hay being transported by livestock is still a common sight in Maramures.

ITALY

97

into chianti country

World-class city • Classic Tuscany • Vineyards galore

With myriad twists and turns coupled with signage that doesn't always do the trick, it is easy to get off course. This isn't a bad thing at all given that most byways lead to pleasures—and road signs pointing to Siena.

Leave Siena (if you can tear yourself away) and head northwest. The countryside, not surprisingly, is awash in vineyards. Castellina in Chianti is a good place to bone up on Tuscan viniculture, purchase some olive oil, and stroll a medieval vaulted street: Via delle Volte. Head east on an especially scenic stretch to Radda in Chianti.

The exquisitely sited 11th-century Vallambrosan abbey, not far from Badia a Coltibuono, now is a restaurant. Continuing southward look for signs announcing Castello di Brolio, reached via a cypress-lined avenue. A highlight of the last leg of the trip is San Gusmè, one of the area's most picturesque villages.

travelwise

Start Siena **End** Siena **Distance** 50 miles (80 km)
Roads Siena is the southernmost point of the trip. Head out going west on the SS2, SR222, SR429, SP408, SP484
Don't Miss Lingering on Siena's shell-shaped Piazza del Campo • Radda in Chianti's medieval core with its age-old archways and crooked lanes • The impressively situated Badia a Coltibuono, one of Tuscany's most venerable monasteries

Abbazia di San Lorenzo, a medieval monastery-turned-villa in Gaiole in Chianti

Celebrating a religious festival in the town of Palazzolo Acreide, energetic musicians parade through the streets.

sicilian loop

Ruins and more ruins • Rural villages • Honey and olive oil

The route weaves through southeast Sicily's rugged limestone mountains—Monti Iblei—known for dynamite views, sleepy villages, and archaeological sites. Leave seaside Syracuse and head west toward Belvedere, stopping at the ruins of 4th-century B.C. Castello Eurialo, from Syracuse's days as a formidable Greek city. Winding roads then lead to Pantalica, Sicily's most important necropolis. From the mountain hamlet of Buccheri, take the ridgetop road to Vizzini (stop to see the churches), then onto Giarratana (more worthwhile churches). A minor road takes you almost to the summit of Monte Lauro (3,234 feet, 986 m), the Iblei's highest point.

The village of Palazzolo Acreide shows off fine baroque buildings and Sicilian rural life in an excellent museum. The nearby ruins of Akrae highlight the area's ancient past. For another taste of rural life, take a side trip to Buscemi to see the entertaining and informative ethnological exhibits.

travelwise

Start Syracuse **End** Syracuse **Distance** 110 miles (177 km) plus 20 miles (32 km) for detours

Roads Local roads and S124

Insider Tip In addition to a restaurant (in a restored shepherd's cottage), the Pantalica Ranch accommodates overnight guests and offers horseback trips.

An almond tree with violet blooms provides a colorful addition to the landscape near Berkane.

MOROCCO

above zegzel gorge

Spectacular gorge scenery • Mountain views • Citrus and olive groves

East of the Rif mountain ranges is Zegzel Gorge—one of the country's most dramatic. Sheer rock faces, olive and citrus trees, and the fast-flowing Oued Zegzel impress even the most jaded traveler. Drive about 2 miles (3 km) before reaching the Zegzel Gorge. After some 5 miles (8 km), the valley views become grand.

Continue to Grotte de Chameau. This large cave complex, closed for several years due to flood damage, provides a nice place to stop and ogle the crystal-clear waters of an Oued Zegzel tributary. Gazing upward you'll see the towering form of Jebel Tafoughalt, one of the highest peaks in the Beni Snassen range. Farther on, the valley opens to a bowl-shaped area with terraced farm plots. After a stretch of switchbacks you'll reach Grotte des Pigeons, where skeletal remains of early Stone Age birds and humans have been found. Heading south to Taforalt, start thinking about the good food that awaits in this town's northern end.

travelwise

Start Berkane **End** Taforalt **Distance** 24 miles (39 km)
Roads The main N2 highway, local roads
Don't Miss Tasting the locally grown kumquats—favored by the ancient Romans • Picnicking in the hamlet of Zegzel, next to a river gushing from a cliff • Eating a clementine in Berkane, acknowledged to be Morocco's citrus capital

the old silk road

Old cities • Towering minarets • Turquoise-domed mosques

Though a magic carpet seems more appropriate, it will be a gas-powered vehicle—rent one at Tashkent's international airport—that transports you into the past. Strung between China and the Mediterranean Sea, the Silk Road was in truth several byways. Some of the trading centers along the way evolved into cities where you still can witness time-honored craftsmanship and works of art.

Ethereal and spacious, Samarqand is such a place—one of the world's oldest cities, founded more than 2,750 years ago. Though there is much that is modern, historic landmarks remain, among them the stunning mosque of Bibi-Khanom.

From Samarqand, the road to the medieval city of Bukhara bisects a landscape of wooded hills and pastures. The Ark of Bukhara—the city's massive ancient fort—looms like an artificial mountain. Nearby, the 12th-century Kalyan Minaret—155 feet (47 meters)—was mighty tall for its time. Wind things up in Khiwa, where 19th-century buildings stand on ancient foundations.

travelwise

Start Tashkent **End** Khiwa **Distance** 745 miles (1,199 km)
Roads M39, M37, A380
Insider Tip In Bukhara, head to the Amulet Hotel, as authentic as it gets and conveniently located in the center of the ancient city.

Sky blue domes on the minarets of the Chor-Minor Madrassah bring it a unique charm.

JAPAN

101

osado skyline drive

Green-mountain panoramas
• Fishing ports • Good hiking

A trip that can be undertaken only in May through October (because of weather, the road is closed the rest of the year), this Sado Island sojourn starts with a car ferry trip to Ryotsu. Once back on land, you drive to Chigusa, where the Osado Skyline route officially begins.

Along this modern ribbon of road that slices through the mountains, you are treated to grand views of remote Sado (Japan's sixth largest island) and the surrounding Sea of Japan. One of the trip's highlights, saved for last, is the former silver- and gold-mining town of Aikawa on the island of Sado's southern coast.

travelwise

Start Chigusa   **End** Sado gold mine
Distance 155 miles (249 km)
Roads B48, B46, B47, B44, local roads
Don't Miss The peak of Kinpokusan (Sado Island's highest peak), reachable via a 90-minute walk (10 miles, 16 km) east of Gortin • A unique bird-watching option: Extinct in the wild, the elegant toki (Japanese crested ibis) has been reintroduced to the island; white and slender, it has a long black beak and a dense crest of plumes at its nape • Sado *nishime,* a simmering pot of tofu, seaweed, radishes, and carrots

The orange sun off Niigata Prefecture on Sado Island illuminates the jagged landscape and the still ocean.

DRIVES BY COUNTRY

ARGENTINA
Along the Salta Loop **48**
Pure Patagonia **107**

AUSTRALIA
Great Ocean Road **35**
The Pacific Highway **60**

BOTSWANA
Wild Okavango **87**

BRAZIL
Along the Green Coast **22**

CAMBODIA
Phnom Penh Ride **59**

CANADA
Cape Breton Circle **10**
Green Gables Shore, Prince
    Edward Island **23**
East from Montreal **40**
A Calgary Circle **41**
Icefields Parkway **64**
Newfoundland Fun **65**
Yukon Circle **98**

CHINA
Driving Sai Kung **93**

COLOMBIA
Coffee Country **106**

COSTA RICA
Coastal Adventure **21**
Caribbean Wild **77**

CROATIA
Classic Wine Road,
    Plesivica **108**

CUBA
Cuba's Southwest **101**

CZECH REPUBLIC
The Castle Route **82**
Northern Bohemia **118**

DOMINICAN REPUBLIC
Cordillera Samaná **104**

EGYPT
A West Bank Loop **54**

ENGLAND
London by Bus **51**
A Cotswolds Loop **79**
North York Moors **111**

FRANCE
Three Riviera Roads **30**
Indre River Ride **80**
A "Grand Canyon" **114**

GERMANY
Romantic Road Trip **81**
The Alpine Road **115**

GREECE
Out of Athens **51**
Peloponnesus **85**

GUADELOUPE
Basse-Terre Loop **20**

ICELAND
The Ring Road **25**

INDIA
A Chennai Spin **34**
Discovering Goa **58**

IRELAND
The Ring of Kerry **78**

ITALY
Amalfi Charms **31**
Via Appia Antica **83**
Langhe Valley, Piedmont **108**
Into Chianti Country **120**
Sicilian Loop **121**

JAMAICA
Pirate Path **18**

JAPAN
Osado Skyline Drive **124**

MEXICO
Baja Expedition **75**
Path of the Conquerors,
    Yucatán **83**

MOROCCO
Beyond Fès **55**
Above Zegzel Gorge **122**

THE NETHERLANDS
The Tulip Route **50**

NEW ZEALAND
Coastal East Cape **37**
Driving the Catlins **95**

NORTHERN IRELAND
Sperrin Mountains **109**

NORWAY
Northern Thrills **27**

OMAN
Along a Mideast Coast **56**

PANAMA
Azuero Experience **46**
Along the Cordillera Central **75**
North of Penonomé **105**

PERU
Pan-Am Highway **47**

PHILIPPINES
Cordillera Terraces **90**

PORTUGAL
Strongholds of the Middle
    Ages **108**
Country Roads **112**

PUERTO RICO
The Panoramic Route **102**

ROMANIA
Transylvania Spin **84**
Rural Maramures **119**

RUSSIA
Moscow's Golden Ring **53**

SCOTLAND
Applecross Route **26**
Glasgow to St. Andrews **51**

SOUTH AFRICA
The Garden Route **32**
Wheat Fields and Vineyards,
    Swartland **108**

SPAIN
Spain's Secret Coast **28**
Along High Hills **113**

SWITZERLAND
Looping Lovely Lakes **117**

TAIWAN
Taroko Gorge **92**

TANZANIA
Serengeti Safari **88**

TURKEY
Bosporus Tour **51**

UNITED STATES
Alaska, Seward Highway **72**
Alaska, Yukon Circle **98**
California, Big Sur Coast **16**
California, On John Steinbeck's
    Heels: Monterey County **23**
California, Sunset
    Boulevard **45**
California, Death Valley
    Drive **71**
Florida, Miami to the Keys **43**
Georgia, Chattahoochee! **67**
Hawaii, Hana's Highway,
    Maui **17**
Hawaii, East End Drive **74**
Maine, Maine's Bold Coast **11**
Massachusetts, Old King's
    Highway **12**
Massachusetts, Concord's
    Literary Route **23**
Missouri, Following Twain:
    Hannibal and Environs **23**
Montana, To-the-Sun Road **70**
Montana and
    Wyoming, Beartooth
    Highway **100**
New Mexico and
    Arizona, Route 66 **69**
New York, Down Fifth
    Avenue **42**
North Dakota and South
    Dakota, Following Lewis
    and Clark **83**
Oregon, Pacific Grace **14**
Vermont, Riding Vermont
    100 **66**
Virginia and North
    Carolina, Blue Ridge
    Parkway **99**
Washington, The Western
    Isles **13**

UZBEKISTAN
The Old Silk Road **123**

VIETNAM
Driving the Mandarin Road **83**
Driving the DMZ **89**

THE WORLD'S MOST SCENIC DRIVES 101 SPECTACULAR TRIPS

Produced by the National Geographic Society
1145 17th Street N.W.
Washington, D.C. 20036-4688 U.S.A.

John M. Fahey, Jr., Chairman of the Board and Chief Executive Officer
Timothy T. Kelly, President
Declan Moore, Executive Vice President; President, Publishing
Melina Gerosa Bellows, Executive Vice President; Chief Creative Officer,
Books, Kids, and Family

STAFF FOR THIS BOOK
Anne Alexander, Senior Vice President, Editorial Director
John MacKethan, Vice President, Retail Sales & Special Editions
Jonathan Halling, Design Director, Books and Children's Publishing
Marianne R. Koszorus, Director of Design
Barbara A. Noe, Senior Editor
Bridget A. English, Project Editor
Sheila Buckmaster, Writer
Whitney Jones, Contributing Writer
Meredith Wilcox, Photo Editor
Bob Gray, Designer
Galen Young, Illustrations Specialist
Carl Mehler, Director of Maps
Sven M. Dolling, Michael McNey, and XNR Productions, Map Research
    and Production
R. Gary Colbert, Production Director
Jennifer A. Thornton, Director of Managing Editorial
Judith Klein, Production Editor
Lisa A. Walker, Production Project Manager
Robert L. Barr, Manager, Manufacturing and Quality Management

For more information about NGS, please call 1-800-NGS-LINE
(647-5463) or visit us online at www.nationalgeographic.com/
books.

To order this or other National Geographic Collectors Editions,
please call 1-800-777-2800 or visit us online at http://ngm
.nationalgeographic.com/special-editions/special-editions.

Material used in this book is drawn from the following National
Geographic Society publications: National Geographic *Traveler* guide-
book series; National Geographic Driving Guide to America series;
National Geographic *Guide to Scenic Highways and Byways;* National
Geographic *Traveler* "Tours of a Lifetime": October 2007, May/June
2008; National Geographic *Traveler* "50 Places of a Lifetime": October
1999, October 2009; National Geographic *Traveler* "Oman's Secret
Coast," October 2006

ISBN 978-1-4351-5281-6 (hardcover)

This 2014 edition printed for Barnes & Noble, Inc. by the National
Geographic Society.

Printed in Hong Kong

14/THK/1